GW01425298

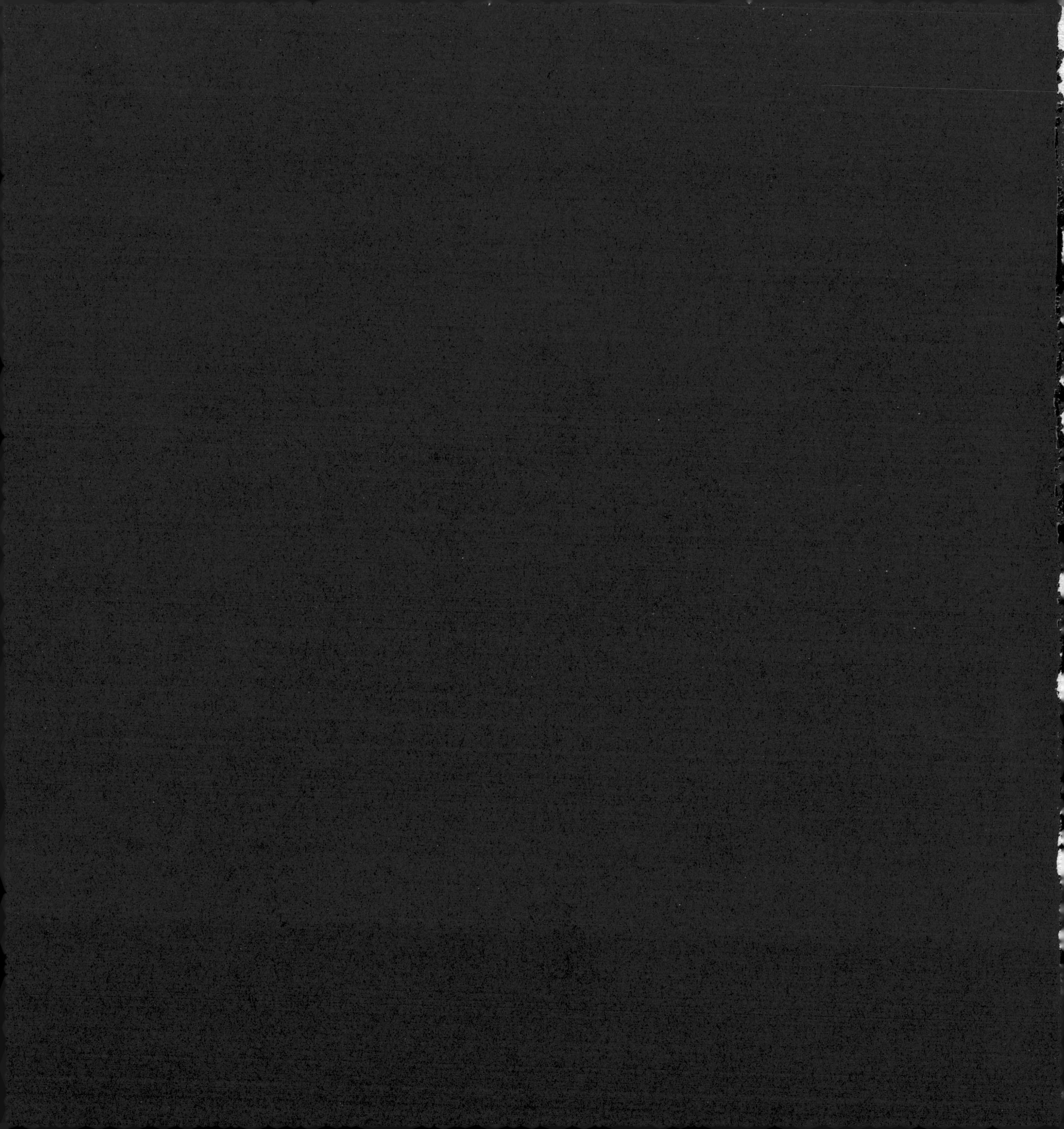

Autodrome

The lost race circuits of Europe

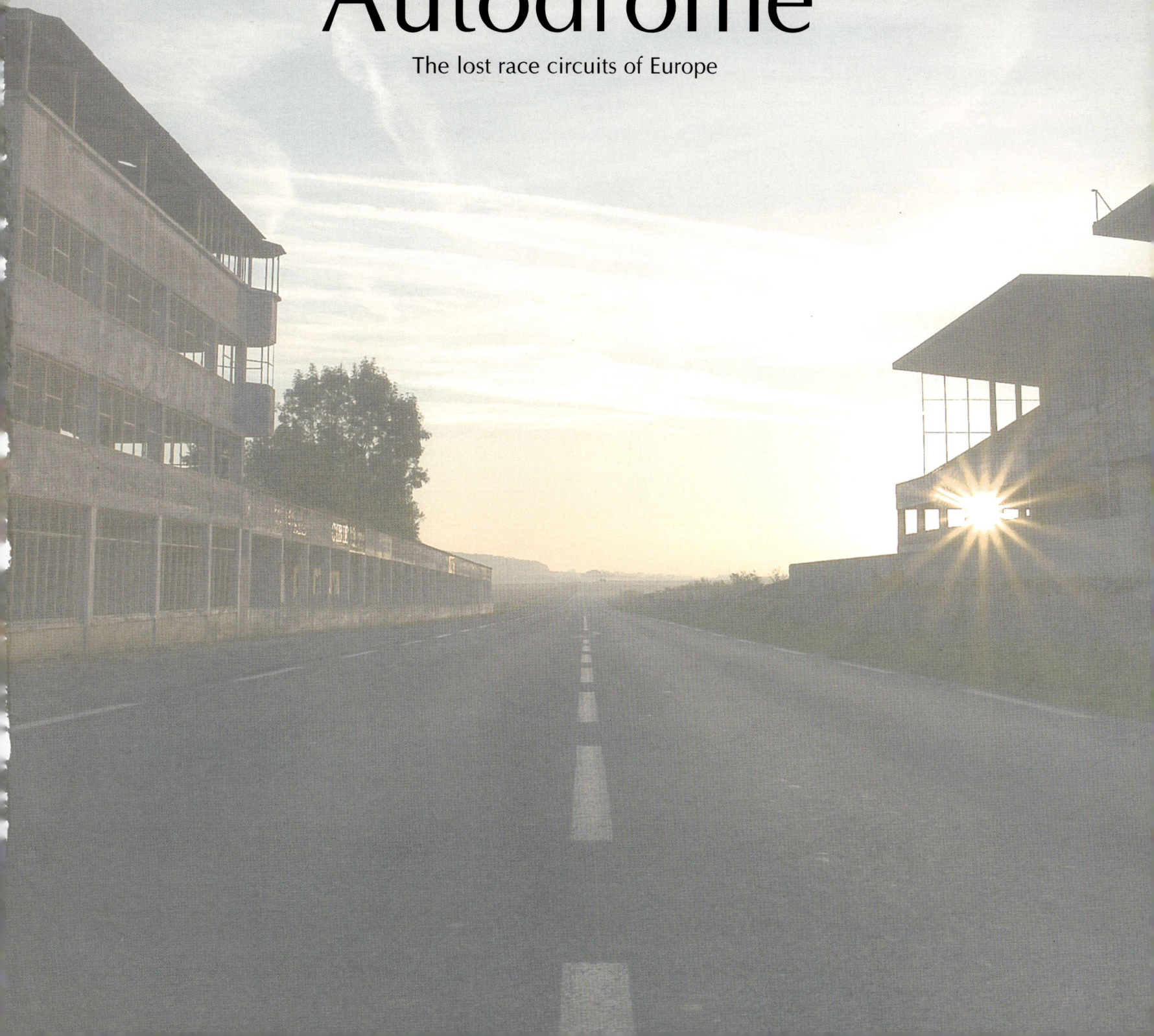

Also from Veloce Publishing –

First published in 2005 by Veloce Publishing Limited, 33 Trinity Street, Dorchester DT1 1TT, England. Fax 01305 268864/e-mail info@veloce.co.uk/web www.veloce.co.uk or www.velocebooks.com. Reprinted December 2005.

ISBN: 1-904788-31-9/ISBN 13: 978-1-904788-31-7/UPC: 6-36847-00331-9

Printed in Italy by D'Auria Industrie Grafiche.

Autodrome

The lost race circuits of Europe

S.S. Collins & Gavin D. Ireland

VELOCE PUBLISHING
THE PUBLISHER OF FINE AUTOMOTIVE BOOKS

About this book and acknowledgements

The Internet had a lot to do with the idea for this book; in forums various tracks and circuits were discussed and the question often asked: what remained of the track today? Every now and again somebody would post an evocative image of a piece of crumbling banking or a faded advertising hoarding.

After seeing pictures of that great memorial to those halcyon days that lies near Reims, I decided I had to see it for myself. Living in sight of Crystal Palace I knew of the remnants of that track, and Brooklands. A holiday in the Czech Republic resulted in a visit to the Masarykring. There and then I decided to visit all of Europe's lost circuits and write a text about not only the history of the venues, but also what remains of them today. This would be combined with a sort of travel report or guide based on my own experiences.

As you will see, photography is a big part of this book. I decided to try and find as many previously unseen and unpublished period pictures as I could, and also take some stunning modern images myself. This last bit was a problem, however, as I'm simply not capable of taking stunning images of any type – I'm not even always capable of taking any type of image! Those pictures I did have which I intended to send to the publishers I rather stupidly exposed to daylight, forgetting that the camera was loaded ...

I needed help, and that came in the form of a talented young photographer by the name of Gavin Ireland, who agreed to help out and travel with me to the circuits … the fool. Gavin had taken some excellent shots to accompany an article I had written on the Sports 1000 racing series, which appeared in *Motorsport News*. They were fantastic. I'm sure you will see a lot more of Gavin's work over the next few years.

We had to decide which circuits we would feature. Some were obvious: Brooklands, and Reims – the track which graces the book's front cover, for example – but others took more thought. We had a shortlist of circuits, some of which are mentioned in the following paragraph, together with the reasons why they didn't make it into the book.

Rouen Les Essarts, Le Mans, Donington Park, Dundrod, Spa Franchorchamps, Mettet, Chimay, Solitude, Fribourg, Rest and, be thankful, Dieppe, Monjuich Park and Birmingham. Sitges was included until a very late stage – even featuring in some early mock-up stages. However, the circuit was ultimately dropped as we felt that some of it was not in keeping with the rest of the book. The first circuit out of the running was Rouen Les Essarts. Although once an incredible circuit it's now nothing more than public road, and there is very little left to show that it was ever anything else. This criteria also rules out Montjuich Park, Dieppe and Fribourg, and the same can be said of Mettet and Solitude, both of which have only a small building remaining, not enough to qualify.

Dundrod: an evocative northern Irish venue – but still in use, as once a year bikers gather for the Ulster Grand Prix. We couldn't include circuits that were still in use, so the tough call had to be made to drop Spa Franchorchamps also. Although a large amount of Spa is abandoned Tarmac (mostly public road), there's still an active circuit on a portion of the old course – same goes for Chimay.

The order of the tracks was problematic and we finally settled for putting them in order of closure, from first to last.

Putting this project together has involved much more than I imagined it would, and a lot of people have helped us out along the way, so I'd like to thank a few of them: Paul Fearnley and all at *Motorsport* magazine; *Motorsport News* and *Autosport*. Rod Grainger, Veronica, and all at Veloce; Rob Semmeling, Kaskia Jussi, Martti Alkio, *Helsingan Sonomlat* newspaper, Mary Roche and the ACG, the Brooklands museum, the Crystal Palace museum, Quentin Potherat, the taxi driver at Helsinki airport, Peter Morley, LAT photographic, Peter Valve, Stefan Marjoram, and Tom and Hazel Ireland. Extra special thanks must go to Gavin David Ireland for agreeing to become involved in the first place.

S. S. Collins

AUTODROME

Contents

www.veloce.co.uk

Introduction

Scattered around Europe are rings of crumbling Tarmac which once played host to the high speed theatre of life and death that is motor racing. These are not the great circuits of today's racing, but the venues of yesterday's. Huge, banked cauldrons of empty concrete which were once pounded by monster aeroplane-engined beasts – their engines howling – now lie silent, grass growing up through the cracks in the track.

Sinuous mountain and parkland circuits swoop between trees and through fields; some have had new circuits built on them, whilst others have been converted into public roads. Abandoned grandstands and timing boxes wait patiently after a long-finished race; all now relics, full of ghosts of the past.

Standing on the banking at Monza or Brooklands, or peering through the trees at Crystal Palace or Brno, these ghosts are palpable: you can almost see Bira in Romulus rushing down the glade with Dobson and Mays in hot pursuit, whilst up on Brooklands' Byfleet banking you expect to see John Cobb fly past in the Napier Railton; while the the hairs on the back of neck stand up as Percy Lambert strides past.

These circuits are very much alive in the memories of those who were there, and by reputation for those too young to have been. Most are now abandoned; left to the elements, and under threat of demolition or redevelopment. I felt now was the time to remember these great edifices, these Autodromes, hosts and playgrounds to the great God Speed.

Of the circuits considered (all European) many were deemed not interesting, complete, or significant enough for inclusion in this book. What we have here, then, are the nine venues that we consider to be the greatest abandoned circuits.

These are the Autodromes.

They all lived.
The Autodromes were alive, each had a soul and each a personality. They brought joy to millions all around the world, love was discovered here, lovers were lost, and sometimes so were lives. Perhaps too much was lost, the price just too high; whichever, the lifeblood that fuelled these great places slowly seeped away and lifeless corpses are all that remain.
This book is not dedicated to any single person or place, but to those who lived with the circuits, those who died on them – and the tracks themselves.

Photographer's Introduction

The photography for this book has been an enormous privilege. To climb the banking of Brooklands, or watch the evening sun fade on the Reims podium where Wimille, Caracciola, Fangio and Clark once stood, is to feel the very heartbeat of motor racing.

Linking the nine chosen circuits is this ability to stir the emotions of those even vaguely aware of their past glory. Some – the Nürburgring Sudschleife, Keimola – are more obscure than others, but no less enthralling for it. The Eiffel track always in the shadow of the legendary Nordschleife; the long-forgotten Finnish venue's short history as varied as any circuit in the world.

Then there are the truly epic battlegrounds of motor racing history. AVUS, so chilling in its simple purpose; Monza, where one can sit in the forest with Le Mans prototypes racing on the current circuit, fully expectant that their 1950s equivalents will come roaring around the banking at any moment.

Most moving of all was to watch the final races at L'Autodrome de Linas-Montlhéry, and stand as another great and historic track slipped out of life and into history.

In the very last photograph of the book is a blemish, an imperfection. The speck on Montlhéry's distant banking is a moped-bound security guard who, shortly after I shot my last image of the doomed track, instructed me that it was too dangerous to be on any part of the banking, despite it remaining solid after more than seventy years. This fastidious, institutionalised aversion to risk is perhaps allegorical of the closure of some of these circuits, and the continued emasculation of many more tracks across Europe. Few would welcome a return to the lethal dangers posed by these circuits in their day, but surely there is some middle ground between the caged spectator enclosures and basic corners of today, and the thrilling intimacy of these autodromes?

I would encourage all who read this book to visit these monumental tracks before they disappear entirely, and support the efforts to preserve them. Nigel Roebuck has written of Formula One that he can think of no other sport with such little regard for its heritage. I hope that this proves untrue of motor racing in general, as these circuits are ingrained with the history of the sport. They still resonate with a passion that is the lifeblood of racing. If my photographs can convey even a fraction of this, they will have succeeded in their aim.

Gavin D. Ireland

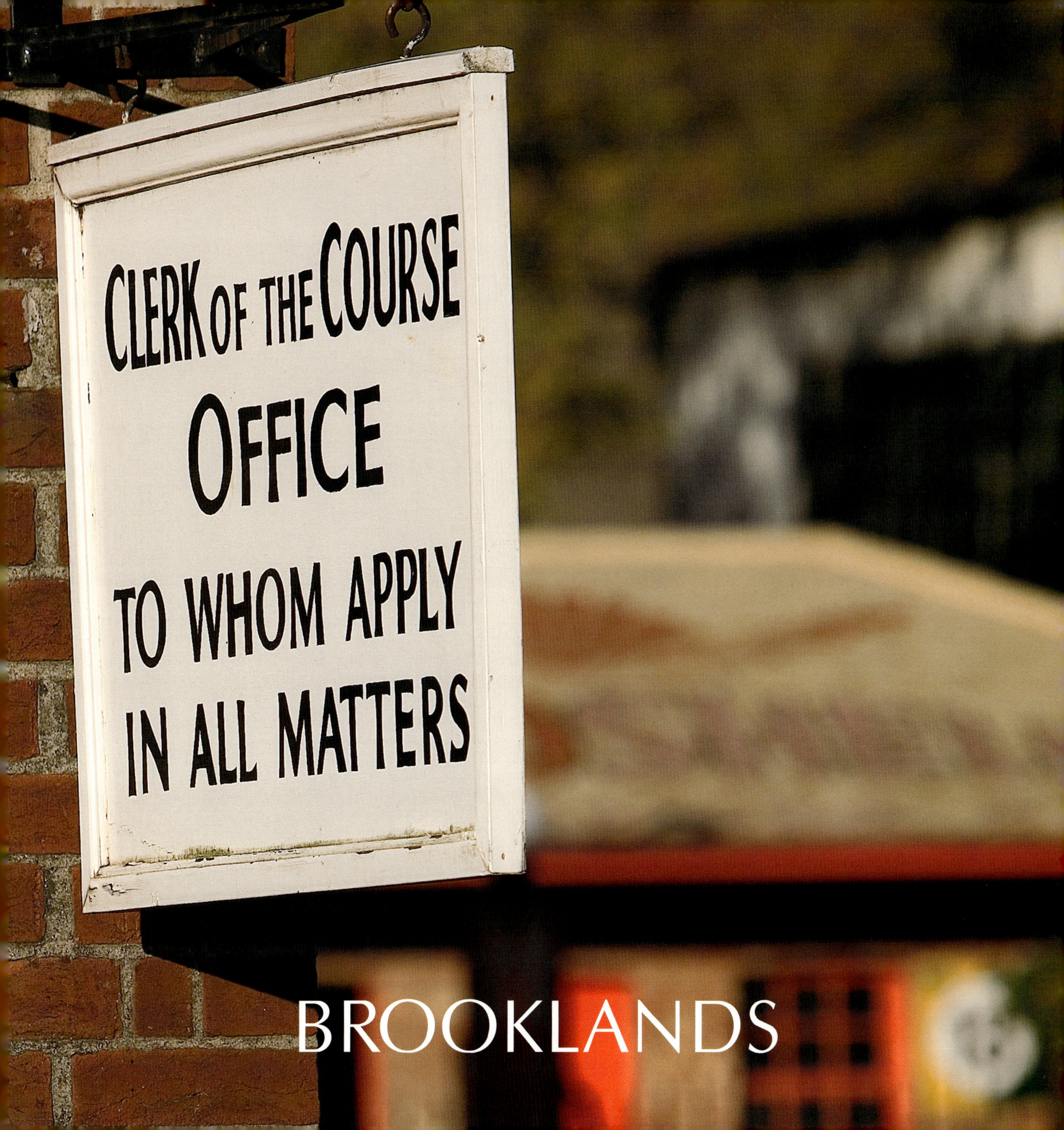

CLERK OF THE COURSE
OFFICE
TO WHOM APPLY
IN ALL MATTERS

BROOKLANDS

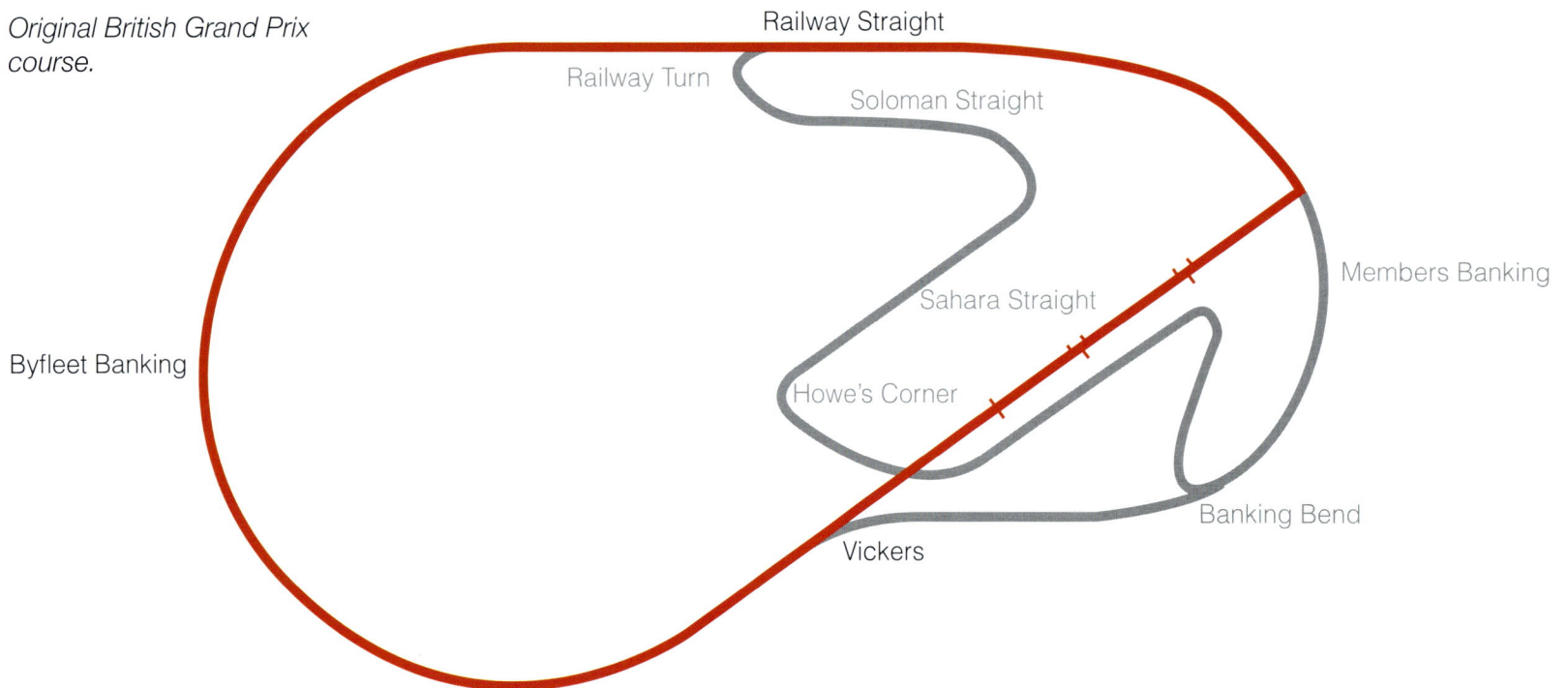

Original British Grand Prix course.

Railway Straight

Railway Turn

Soloman Straight

Members Banking

Sahara Straight

Byfleet Banking

Howe's Corner

Banking Bend

Vickers

Trains rattle past the old straight, carrying commuters on their interminable trudge from the Surrey towns of Woking and Guildford toward London. En route the sharp-eyed amongst them will have noticed a collection of apparently abandoned aeroplanes; there is a large building site nearby, where work is well under way on a short circuit, but the commuters are unlikely to know that. They are too busy thinking about integrated management accounts to realise that they're flashing past an area where wheels once seemed to sprout wings.

Before Brooklands there were no autodromes; nothing but the odd event on temporary circuits, such as the one at nearby Crystal Palace. As far as motor racing circuits go Brooklands is the Genesis; prior to this pre-existing paths and roads – built for uses other than motorsport – had been used.

The history of Brooklands begins in 1906 in Sicily. Motoring enthusiast Hugh Fortescue Locke-King watched the Targa Florio race that year, and later the French Grand Prix, neither of which had any British entries. The reason for this, Locke-King surmised, was that as the UK was stifled by a blanket 20mph speed limit, there was no way a British manufacturer could compete without having access to a permanent test and race venue. Locke-King called together to Weybridge in Surrey all those of like mind and thrashed out a plan.

Nine months of hard work, river diversion, and railway building later it was ready. At 3.25 miles (5.23km) long, the world's first purpose-built motor circuit was finished. Roughly oval in shape, the outer circuit was wide and fast; it had two unique, huge banked corners at each end, the longer and less banked of which was known as the Byfleet Banking, the steeper, shorter banking near the paddock and race HQ the exclusive Members Banking. The entire venue was set up like a horse racing circuit with a starting and finishing straight cutting its way between a kink in the track at the 'fork' to the Members Banking. John Cobb, who is synonymous with Brooklands, described a run around the track in the 1939 book *Motor Racing*:

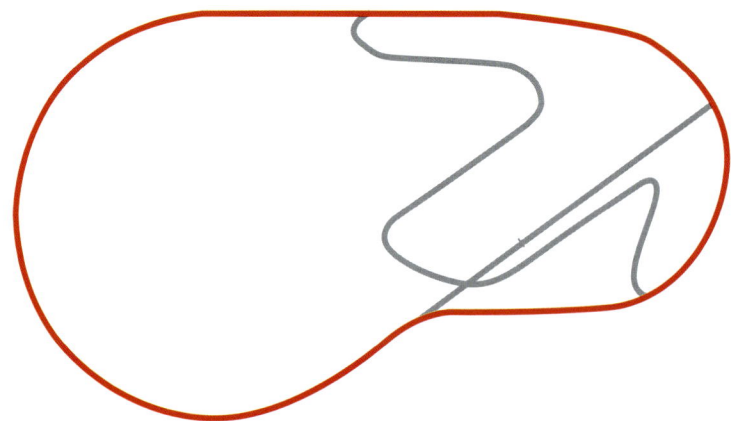

The outer circuit.

Brooklands was the first home of the British Grand Prix. The scene here is the start of the 1926 race. (Courtesy LAT)

"You cannot take a really fast car on full throttle right round Brooklands, since quite apart from the difficulties of the Byfleet Banking and the Members Banking there is a quite unbanked curve round the Vickers Shed which is not at all easy to tackle at full speed. This curve, as a matter of fact, is made more difficult because the driver of a car coming fast off the slope of the Byfleet Banking cannot see clearly around the turn, which means that if the car is travelling at 150mph (241kph) or more, and another slower, unseen car is on the curve but close to the shed, the situation becomes very difficult for the driver of the faster car.

"The turn itself has to be judged very like a turn of equal radius on the road. The ease with which the car goes round depends to no little extent on exactly where one leaves the preceding Byfleet Banking, added to which, if the wind is in a certain direction, it seems to bounce off the side of the Vickers Shed and tends to push a fast car towards the inner edge of the track.

"The run onto the Home Banking is comparatively easy, though again it is necessary to select the right position of entry, and a car's width up or down will make all the difference to the turn; but once on the banking the driver's difficulties are not ended, for in a matter of fifty yards or so there is a most peculiar portion of the track. Quite what is the matter nobody seems to know. There is no bad bump, the radius of the turn does not seem to alter, but at this precise spot the car tends to swerve up or down in a manner which is most alarming when first encountered, and it is extremely difficult to cross this point at any time with the throttle wide open. This particular point in the track takes every bit as much knowing as a corner on the road.

"Further on the car is sheltered by the Members Hill, as it runs round the top of the Home Banking, but this has its drawbacks because the machine comes out from under the Members Bridge just where the hill ceases, and if the wind is blowing in a certain direction it tends to make the car swerve towards the top of the banking.

"A little further still there is another problem. As the Home Banking sweeps down to the Railway Straight it crosses over a bridge straddling the River Wey. Possibly this bridge has settled somewhat; in all events the track suddenly slopes downwards, and a section of it resembles a hump-backed bridge, becoming more humped towards the top of the banking, cutting the corner, as it were, onto the Railway Straight, the bump, though bad was not appalling. If, on the other hand, the car has to run at full speed near the top of the banking at this point, it leaps into the air for a very considerable distance, and alights onto the Railway Straight with a crash which certainly does no good to the mechanism."

The first Brooklands events took place in mid-1907, and were publicly hailed a success, but Brooklands really suffered from a fair few teething troubles in the first few years of its existence, including low entries for races and, more worryingly, low spectator turnout. Prophecies of complete fiasco, bandied about at the time of the circuit's conception, looked like becoming reality. Spectators complained that the vast nature of the venue made it hard to follow the races, and car identification was difficult as the only way to do this was by the drivers' jockey-like coloured silks. This situation did not change until 1909 when A. V. Ebblewhite persuaded the Brooklands Automobile Club to feature numbers on the sides of competing cars.

At the beginning of the 1908 season a meeting was held at the track for amateur drivers; lap times were taken in the morning and the race run in the afternoon on a handicap system. Eleven competitors started and seven finished within the same one-and-three-quarter minute period: the race was won by just ten yards. This was an exciting race and the Brooklands executive noted this.

A private competitor list was drawn up, along with a set of regulations which included the following:

• A private competitor shall have no direct interest in the automobile or accessory industries.

• A private competitor shall neither enter, nor drive in any race at Brooklands a vehicle which is the property of a person or persons having a direct interest in the automobile or accessory industries.

• A private competitor shall not accept any fee or remuneration of any kind, whether direct or indirect from any firm or individual for driving or entering a motor car in any race or competition.

• A private competitor shall be entitled to enter for and drive in races, even though, by their conditions, the races be open to others beside private competitors, but in races for private competitors they alone shall be eligible to compete.

This set of regulations – along with the 1908 amateurs' meeting – is most certainly the root of British club racing, and also, perhaps, made motor racing a sport rather than the science that the top level of competition always was and has been since.

Regular meetings regarding racing events and also speed record attempts took place on the circuit. S. F. Edge set a 24 hour speed record of almost 66mph/1581 miles (106.216kph/2544.303km). In 1913 Percy Lambert set the outer circuit speed record. Lambert achieved a 103.84mph (167.10kph) lap but felt he could go faster, so a few months later made another attempt on the record, which he promised his worried fiancée would be his last ever as it was due to take place a very short time before their wedding. The attempt was indeed his last as during it he crashed and was killed.

The outbreak of war in 1914 effectively closed the circuit for six years although it did try to carry on regardless; the last prewar meeting occurred the day before the outbreak of hostilities. During the war in 1915 two motorcycle race meetings were held; 'All Khaki' and 'United Services'. After the armistice it took

Locke-King until 1920 to restore the venue to good order after the solid tyres of military vehicles had played havoc with the circuit surface.

The Junior Car Club held the first of its famous 200 mile classics, and Malcolm Campbell made a return after serving in the army, but the race was won by another now familiar name; Henry Seagrave in a Talbot.

Brooklands is the original home of the British Grand Prix (an event later held at Brands Hatch, Aintree, and currently Silverstone). The inaugural event took place in August of 1926 but, because the outer circuit was deemed not quite right for Grand Prix competition, steps were taken to make the course more continental. As a result two chicanes – temporary and made out of sandbanks – were added onto the end of the finishing straight. The track then joined the Members Banking, turning anti-clockwise and following the outer circuit along the Railway Straight, then round the Byfleet Banking which joined the finishing straight. 14 entries were received: a good field at the

time. 9 cars took the start, three Talbots, three Delages, Malcolm Campbell in a Bugatti, George Eyston in his Aston Martin, and Frank Halford's Halford Special. After 110 laps of the 2.6 mile (4.18km) course Robert Senechal and Louis Wagner emerged victorious in their Delage.

The outer circuit record was hotly contested over the years, and speeds increased rapidly. Kaye Don won the *Daily Herald Trophy* (awarded by the paper for fastest driver around the track) in a close fight with 'Tim' Birkin, Kaye's Sunbeam lapping at 137.58mph (221.40kph). In 1932 Birkin snatched the record in his red blower Bentley, clocking 137.96mph (222.09kph). More was to come, however. An almighty scrap ensued for outer circuit superiority; John Cobb won out in the end, lapping at 143mph (230.1kph) in the Napier-Railton. His car remains at the track's museum, maintained in fully working condition.

A new clerk of the course was appointed in 1930, Percy Bradley invented another course layout for Brooklands, the 'Mountain' circuit. Simply, it ran up onto the Members Banking from the finishing straight, followed it clockwise down to the fork, then hard right up the finishing straight. The short fast track measured 1.25 miles (2.01k). During a 1936 race run on the Mountain circuit Raymond Mays established the mountain course record at 84.31mph (135.68kph).

Another configuration of Brooklands was used for the first 'International Trophy'. A 3.369 mile (5.421km) course was used, and the rolling start occurred on the Railway Straight, with cars running round the Members Banking and onto the finishing straight. At the end of the straight a left-handed hairpin on a link section ran up to the foot of the test hill, from where the course took a right-hand hairpin through a bit of a wiggle and rejoined the Members Banking towards its conclusion. The cars would then run down to the fork and onto the Members Banking.

Between 1907 and 1937 Brooklands really was the home of motor racing in Britain, but in the 1930s it faced some stiff competition from the road circuit at Donington Park and the return of Crystal Palace to the motorsport scene. The Brooklands Automobile Racing Club responded to these road course upstarts by constructing one of its own. The new circuit ran its first race on 1st May 1937.

Prince Chula Chakrabongse of Siam entered his younger cousin Bira in the first race. He describes the new course in his 1939 book *Road Star Hat Trick*.

The designers of the Campbell circuit had good spectator visibility in mind, and in this they succeeded admirably. Whether the circuit truly resembled real road racing conditions has since been the subject of much debate. The new circuit is of the 'road-cum-track' variety as at Montlhéry in France, though here there was much less road. There's now a road which runs parallel to the old finishing straight on the opposite side of the paddock, and it's here that the start is located, at the end of the line of excellent concrete pits, with a deck for spectators as at the Nürburgring.

From the start the road runs towards the test hill, where there is a sharp turn to the right (Test Hill Hairpin). The road skirts the hill until it joins the track at a sharp left-hand corner (Banking Bend), then takes in a fast stretch known as 'flat out blind' along the banking of the track until it descends into the Railway Straight. Here, near the sewage farm, there's a sharp left-hand corner (Railway Turns) and the new road begins, running parallel with the Railway Straight, turning right (Aerodrome Curve) and going on toward the River Wey (Sahara Straight), which it crosses after a sharp left-hand turn (Howe's Corner). It then crosses the old finishing straight at a slant and joins the pits. This interesting circuit, which measures 2.267 miles (3.648km), can be seen almost in its entirety from the Members Hill.

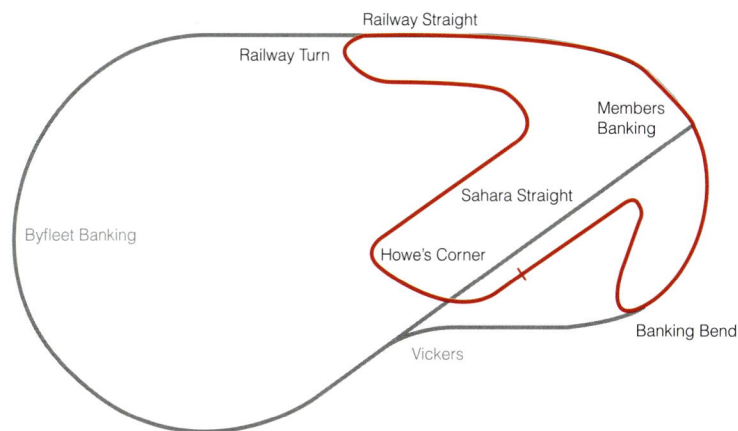

The Campbell circuit.

Action at the Test Hill Hairpin during the Dunlop Jubilee International; Test Hill can be seen to the left of the picture. (Courtesy LAT)

The first race run on the new track was organised by the Brooklands Automobile Racing Club, and was the Campbell Trophy race: 100 laps, 226 miles (363.7km), and open to cars of any capacity. The fastest practice time of 1m 53secs was set by Walker aboard an ERA. A good grid took the start, with entries ranging from Bira in the big Maserati, to a gaggle of 1500cc ERAs.

A memorable dice between Bira and Lord Howe took place but ended badly with Howe suffering a rather nasty shunt as his car hit the parapet of the bridge over the River Wey. The peer was thrown clear and broke some ribs, though, happily, made a full recovery and returned to motor racing. Bira went on to win the race in the Maserati.

The Campbell circuit was a late addition to Brooklands. Here, Alfa Romeo leads ERA and Maserati as Members Hill looks on. (Courtesy LAT)

In 1939 the circuit closed for the duration of World War 2, and was used instead by Hawker and Vickers to build combat aircraft. A slice was cut out of the Byfleet Banking to allow access from Oyster Lane.

After the war there were moves to reopen the circuit, but the damage to the aged concrete was considered too severe. Vickers took over the site and motorsport left Brooklands. But, as with many of the circuits featured in this text, that wasn't quite the end of the story ...

In 1991 a museum opened to celebrate the history of Brooklands, preserving some of the venue's features, and collecting a number of interesting motor cars and aircraft. A few

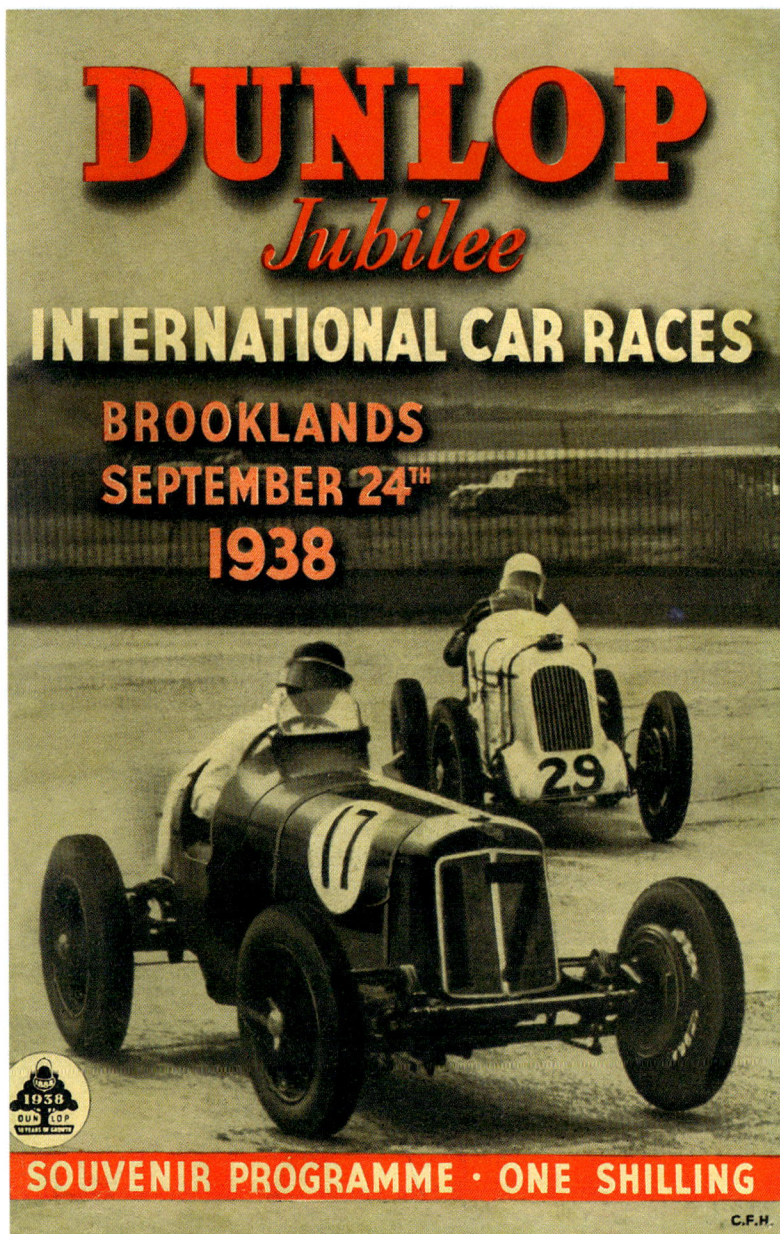

Programme cover for the Dunlop Jubilee International.

Programme cover (Race Card) for the October 15 meeting, which featured races on the outer circuit, Campbell and Mountain circuits. Note "... the right crowd and no crowding".

years later the 750 Motor Club held a sprint on the main runway which ran parallel to the Sahara Straight. It was a far cry from the track's heyday; cars threaded their way round a sea of cones and the event could have been on any disused airfield. The only part of the old course that was used was at the Members end of the Railway Straight, which formed part of the paddock.

... and now

Our sports history is not well maintained in Britain. Today, Brooklands is a jumble of assorted chunks of crumbling bits of banking and abandoned tracks. Recently Daimler-Benz bought a 105 acre chunk of the site for just £5,000,000, on which will be built a test track and technology centre which will "Keep the

on one side of the road is a large Tesco supermarket; on the other, the derelict sweep of the Byfleet Banking. Weeds pushing their way up between the cracks in it, the public road that runs past the supermarket and alongside the Byfleet Banking turns left and cleaves a way through the old track. At this point in the banking the name 'Brooklands' has been cut into the concrete.

On the far side of the road the old banking continues, totally overgrown but with trees marking its passage through the estate. An unfriendly fence discourages passers-by and people exploring the remains from investigating further.

Behind Tesco lies a large chunk of the overgrown banking, hidden from public gaze as it skirts past the industrial units built along its inner perimeter. The back of the banking is fenced off to deter unwanted guests. A security guard pauses to watch us; a small rabbit emerges from higher up the banking and hops away toward Tesco over the overgrown concrete and through the weeds. Drops of rain finally begin to fall from the leaden sky. Brooklands is a moody place ...

Taking the train from Byfleet and New Haw reveals a little more, not only about the poor state of Britain's railways, but also about the Railway Straight. Looking out of the window it's clear that the industrial estate has eaten into massive chunks of the venue. A hanger – similar to that which sits on the start/finish line – also resides on the straight, whilst the rest of the area has become a forgotten car park for forgotten cars and vans. On closer investigation one of these cars seemed pretty much in mint condition – except for the moss growing over it and the family of rabbits living under it.

Whilst the other circuit in London's suburbs, Crystal Palace, has an aura of sad abandonment, Brooklands suggests only waste. Good cars sit rotting slowly on the slowly rotting remnants of a once great circuit. The end of the Railway Straight is intact up to the start of the Members Banking but the section that crossed the Wey is gone.

In the other direction is more of the circuit, and hidden away nearby another large portion of abandoned banking. This section of the Byfleet Banking is great and so very evocative of how the place must once have been. Much of the 'high' groove is covered in thick moss, the surface broken up by contant exposure to the elements and zero maintainance since the start

spirit of Brooklands alive". The local council has approved the development – now only time will tell if Brooklands will once again ring to the sound of highly tuned racing engines.

Driving up the A3, Brooklands is clearly signposted – Brooklands industrial estate, that is; a much smaller sign shows the way to the Brooklands museum.

Following the signs through the leafy Surrey suburbs you reach a mini roundabout and turn right. A strange sight awaits:

of the Second World War. Daimler Chrysler – the area's new owner – is developing the area into a park, it is claimed. The park would, if built, be a strange place; swings and manicured grassy areas overlooked by the brooding hulk of the banking, silently waiting for a race that may never again be run.

In the centre of the venue, near the museum area, parts of the Campbell circuit could be identified until the building work began. Standing at aerodrome curve it was possible to drive down the Sahara Straight, albeit badly broken and extremely rough. Howe's Corner was intact, too, as was the bridge over the Wey where a certain individual had the big accident that gave the corner its name. A group of empty office buildings stands alongside the old finishing straight, now a large speed hump-riddled car park. Small trees mark the original width of the track.

The track reappears at the Test Hill Hairpin, now on the edge of the museum complex, the run down to Banking Bend, the access road to the museum. Elements of the Sahara Straight and Aerodrome Curve are included as part of the Daimler Chrysler test track which, by the time this book is published, will have been completed, as work is fully under way on the new facility.

A trip to the museum area is well worthwhile. Some of the pictures in this book show the great collection of Brooklands memorabilia there, which ranges from cars to trinkets, world land speed record-breaking machines and Modern F1 to Indycar machinery. Also present are reminders of Brooklands' aeronautical history; significant aircraft with connections to Brooklands from a prototype Harrier jump jet to Concorde. Enthusiastic staff members give guided tours of the Harrier jump jet, and the interior of a Wellington bomber. Two particular stars are the silver Napier-Railton which will forever hold the outer circuit record, and 'BABS', the car that took the life of J. G. Parry Thomas on Pendine Sands.

The real treat, however, is the semi-preserved section of the Members Banking; even the run down to the finishing straight remains! The twin tunnels under the banking are complete and one can be entered: though there's little to see there's much to feel as the atmosphere is tangible. A restaurant sitting at the top of the Members Hill awaits restoration; it sold its last cream cake to the 'right crowd' in 1939. Perhaps one day the crowd will return. It's rumoured that one of them already has – or perhaps I should say he never left. Many people experience an uncomfortable feeling when standing on the Members Banking near Members Bridge. Few know why but it's been suggested that this may have something to do with Percy Lambert, mentioned previously in the text. During the race in which he died, he ran strongly around the Weybridge track, averaging over 110mph for 120 laps, but as he rounded Members Banking on what became his last lap a rear tyre blew. The massive accident that resulted occurred in the vicinity of Members Bridge: Lambert didn't stand a chance. He was buried at Brompton cemetary in a streamlined coffin that matched his car. Lambert is said to still haunt Members Banking, and the following is an account from a local resident.

"On Halloween one year my older brother went out to a party. I asked him to wake me up when he got back so that we could go out to the race track, which was out the back of our street. Anyway, he woke me up and we went through the woods to the back of the circuit where you can get in through a hole in the fence near the bridge. When we got there we heard footsteps on the bridge, so I climbed up to see who was there but there was no-one around. But the footsteps were still walking and 'cos it's a metal bridge the footsteps were getting louder. Then we heard a car coming round the circuit, which is cut off to cars, so we ran away back through the woods".

This story is not unique as there have been many reported occurrences; doors opening and closing of their own accord, footsteps, revving engines and tyres squealing, all in the dead of night. Some report having heard cars running around the Members Banking, and others have heard a massive smash, yet upon reaching the area the noise came from – almost always near Members Bridge – there's nothing there. There have also been sightings of a figure dressed in white overalls and cloth helmet walking around the car parks that sit on the old track. One young local had to be treated for shock after seeing "... the figure of a man staggering around with his head half hanging off" inside the track. How much truth there is in these tales is debatable. The old track has not yet revealed all its secrets; whether it ever will is uncertain ...

CAMPBELL ROAD

PARRY DRIVE

LOCKE KING ROAD
LEADING TO
BENTLEY DRIVE. EDGE CLOSE.
LOCKE KING CLOSE. SEAGRAVE CLOSE.
JOHN COBB ROAD. CAMPBELL ROAD.
LONSDALE ROAD. SEVEN ARCHES APPROACH.

PARNELL
GARDENS

KAYE DON WAY

JOHN COBB
ROAD

SEGRAVE CLOSE

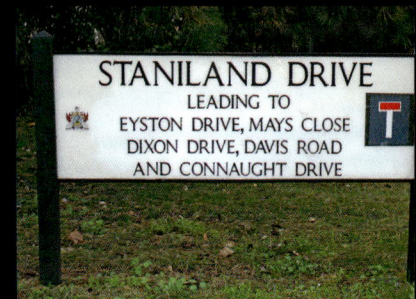

STANILAND DRIVE
LEADING TO
EYSTON DRIVE, MAYS CLOSE
DIXON DRIVE, DAVIS ROAD
AND CONNAUGHT DRIVE

JACKSON

TUNED AND MAINTAINED FOR THE ROAD & TRACK

W. A. CUTHBERT LTD
High St.
GUILDFORD

Agent for
RILEY

DER RING TON
MALDEN
256

(VICTOR DERRINGTON)

MOTOR CYCLE & ACCESSORIES MANUFACTURER

Also at Aero Works
Grafton Road
New Malden
Surrey

PISTONS FOR BUGATTI

Captain A. Frazer-Nash sponsored by His daughters Marion & Joan

MOTOR "BP" SPIRIT

MONZA

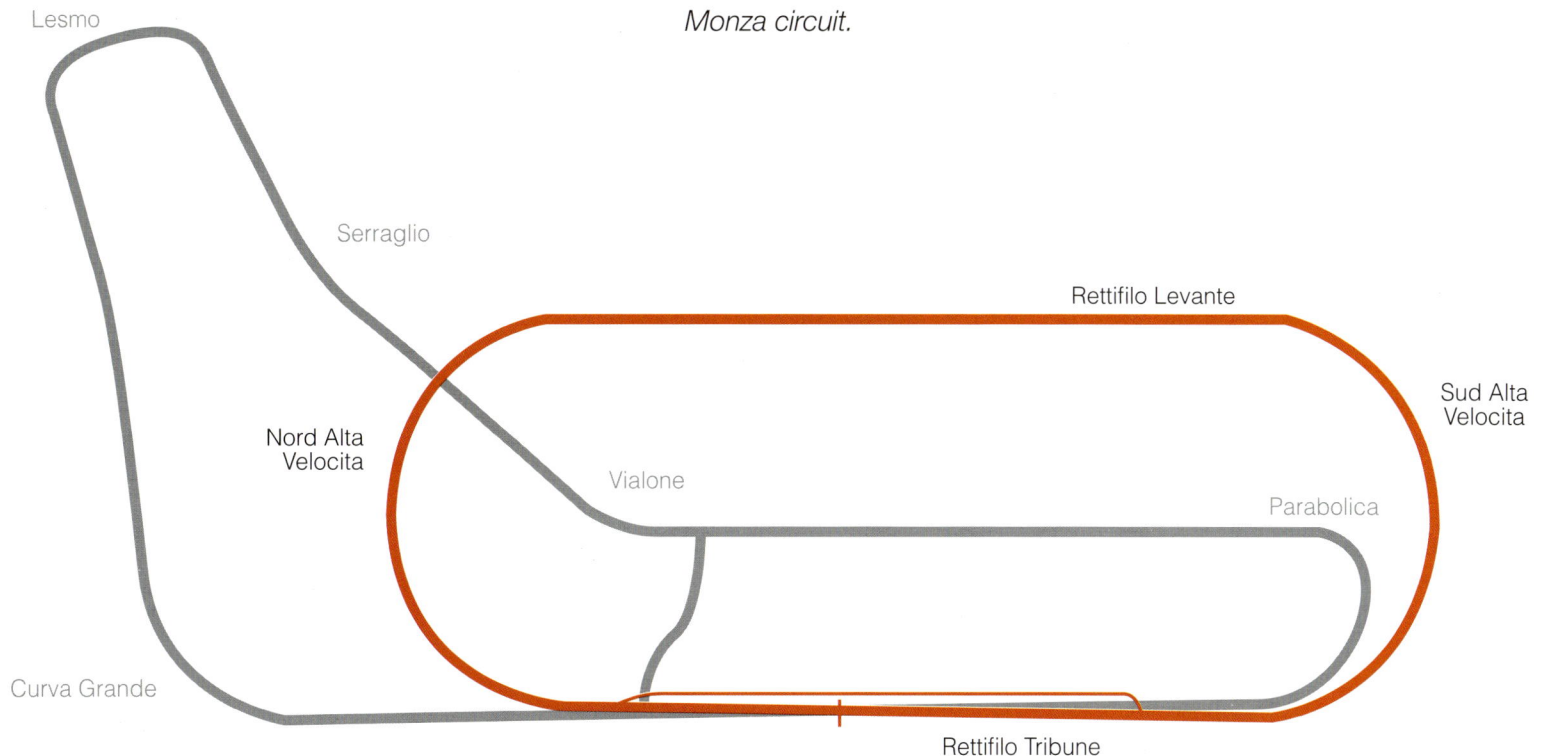

Monza circuit.

Some call it the cauldron of speed, but most call it Monza, home of the Italian Grand Prix, and the fastest circuit on the modern Formula One tour of the globe. It's a modern facility – with a pit and paddock complex that happily accommodates most of the world's top racing series.

Out in the woods that surround this modern autodrome, however, lies something old, almost forgotten: La pista d'alta velocita. If you're lucky you may catch a glimpse of it during TV coverage of the Italian GP. Modern racers speak of it with awe; quietly, in corners in hushed voices. A remnant of a bygone era, when it was plainly dangerous, today it is simply daunting. Racers had a fear of Monza – similar to that reserved for the Nürburgring – because of its combination of very high speeds coupled with almost non-existent safey measures, allied to cars that were deathtraps compared to any modern racer. Death and Monza walked hand-in-hand; Monza was a place where racers died. The 1961 world championship was decided by that fatal pairing when Wolfgang von Trips and a number of spectators lost their lives the day the German count's championship rival, Phil Hill, took the title.

The remnants of 'old' Monza sit in the woods and parkland as a reminder of the dangers today's racing predecessors faced. Such dangers do not sit well with modern racing; perhaps that's why the banking was threatened with demolition in the late 1990s and early 2000s?

Construction of the Monza circuit began in 1922. Although not the only contender, Villa Reale Park was chosen as the venue as it offered a large enclosed area just a short distance from Milan. The planned circuit – designed by architect Alfredo Rosselli – was supposed to be 14km (8.69 miles) in length, but work was almost immediately halted due to "... artistic and monumental value and landscape conservation ..." concerns. The plans were altered and a 10km (6.21 mile) circuit was constructed instead, comprising a high speed ring and a road course (the latter the basis of the current circuit used by the Formula One circus).

Felice Nazzaro and Vincenzo Lancia had already laid the foundation stone when the aforementioned controversy about the circuit's construction erupted. The modified design of the high speed ring was oval in shape; a 4.5km (2.796 mile) route consisting of twin banked curves with a radius of 320 metres (350yds), the banking rising 2.5 metres (2.73yds) from ground level. These turns were linked by two straights, each 1070 metres (1170yds) in length, the pit straight being shared with the longer road course. The tar-coated concrete curves were designed to be taken by the machines of the day at a theoretical top speed of 190kph (118mph). The two straights were made of tar-coated macadam.

On a damp September day in 1922 the circuit was officially opened, and a voiturette race run on the combined 10km (6.21

mile) circuit, won by Pietro Bordino in a Fiat 501. The circuit ran successfully for many years, but technological advances in the cars meant that they quickly outgrew the banked curves, designed for a maximum speed of 190kph (118mph). Cars such as the racing Alfa Romeos, and others of the early to mid 1920s, were easily capable of speeds of around 220kph (136mph), if not higher, and even the bikes were closing on the 200kph (124mph) mark. Just three years into its life the autodromo had become obsolete ...

English racer Earl Howe discusses Monza in the continental circuits chapter of the 1939 book *Motor Racing*:

"A totally different circuit exists in the Royal Park at Monza. Monza is partly a track and partly a road circuit. The principal features are large radius bends with very low banking, which will not permit cars to go round at anything like the speed of which a modern racing car is capable.

"The track is very beautifully laid out and its surroundings are most attractive. There have been many proposals for modifying the track and the races run on it, but so far as I am aware up to the present this has not been done.

"I myself consider the insufficient banking on the two main bends of the track, and the fact that large portions of it run through woods, as its most dangerous features, and I believe that, if it is impossible to provide banking sufficient to take the more powerful racing car at the peak of its performance, it would be better if the banking were done away with altogether. This, however, is merely a personal expression of opinion with which probably many people would not agree. Certain, however, it is that any driver who enters a race at Monza should be a man of great experience, otherwise the way to disaster is easy".

In 1928 tragedy struck Monza. The first ever serious accident in Italian motor racing history occurred when a collision on the main straight during the Italian Grand Prix claimed the lives of driver Emilio Materassi and twenty-seven spectators. The following year the race was run on the high speed course only.

Meanwhile, Vincenzo Florio, president of Italian motorsport's governing body, had been investigating the possibility of creating a new, shorter course. The resultant 'Florio' circuit was made up of the Southern Banking, a short straight, and a pair of ninety degree bends, and had a length of 6.6km (4.1 miles). It was used for both car and bike Grands Prix in 1938.

The full combined circuit was again used for Grand Prix racing in 1932. The ever-present dangers of Monza made their presence felt during the following year's Grand Prix, a day that became known as Black Sunday. A record crowd had turned up at the circuit, fully expecting to see a pair of great races; the Italian Grand Prix on the combined course, and the Monza Grand Prix on the high speed track. A light drizzle greeted fans who watched Luigi Fagioli in an Alfa Romeo, ahead of Maserati star Tazio Nuvolari. There was more racing to come, and most of the top drivers of the day were entered for the Monza GP which consisted of three fourteen lap heats and a final.

The first heat ran without major incident until the ninth lap when the Duesenberg driven by the then president of Scuderia Ferrari, Count Trossi, blew its engine on the Southern Banking. Estimates reported that four gallons of oil were deposited on the track, though it's disputed that Trossi's car problem caused this oil slick. Whatever the cause, it was at this spot that Guy Moll spun badly on the slick, later complaining of the danger to officials.

The grid for the next heat included racing hero Giuseppe Campari, who had elected to sit out the Italian Grand Prix in the morning to concentrate on the afternoon's races. As the cars were pushed up to their grid positions, the Italian ace's appearance was hailed by the partisan crowd. Shouts of "Campari, Campari, Negher, Negher" were received with a wave, the Royal box acknowledged with a fascist salute. (Negher was Campari's nickname due to his very dark skin.) The tanned Italian had just announced his intention to retire from motor racing to become a professional singer.

As the cars waited on the grid, officials coated the oil spill with sand, following Moll's complaints. With the track clear for racing, the starter dropped his flag and the field set off. Baconin Borzacchini led into the first turn with Campari in hot pusuit. The field roared out of sight on the North Banking, and all eyes turned to the exit of the South Curve. Three dots appeared, racing out of the turn, but only three; the front runners had all but vanished! Campari, Borzachinni, Castelbarco and Barbieri were out of the race. The heat continued with just three cars running for 26 minutes, Balestro winning from Pellegrini.

AUTOMOBILE CLUB DI MILANO

L. 50

PROGRAMMA UFFICIALE

Gran premio dell' Autodromo

17 ottobre 1948

Monza

SUPPLEMENTO AL BOLLETTINO INFORMAZIONI N. 4 —

DIRETTORE RESPONSABILE COVACIVICH

ABBINATO ALLA LOTTERIA ITAL...

back was broken when his car rolled and he died soon after arriving at hospital.

The next heat went ahead, two hours delayed, though Giulio Aymini and Piero Taruffi withdrew. It passed with little incident and the grid for the final was readied and started, though shortened by 8 laps. On the ninth tour tragedy struck South Curve for the third time that day, when the car of Bugatti driver and winner of the first heat, Stanislaus Czaikowski, flew off the circuit, landing upside down and well ablaze. Czaikowski was said to have been killed instantly but it's hard to know how bad his injuries were as the fire kept officials back until both car and corpse were completely burnt.

Tazio Nuvolari had withdrawn from the afternoon's race due to tyre trouble, but if he had competed there's little doubt that the 'Flying Mantuan' would have been a front runner and therefore caught up in the chaos. As it was he lost two close associates that day, and spent the night by the side of the corpse of his friend Borzacchini.

Following Black Sunday the speed course was abandoned as a viable race circuit, though parts were still used during some of the following year's races. Another reaction was to seek alternative track layouts, and in 1934 a short track using the Southern Banking, the 'Florio' circuit link and a makeshift hairpin on the start/finish straight was devised. On other layouts chicanes considerably slowed the circuit.

Shortly before the second world war began facilities at the circuit were upgraded with a new main grandstand (2000 capacity), facilities for timekeepers, and a restaurant at ground level. New pits were constructed, and many other facilities and buildings were added or improved. However, before the improved circuit could host any major events the war intervened, though the new facilities were used during the conflict, housing the public automobile registry offices, the offices of the Milan Automobile club and, at one point, animals from Milan zoo!

In 1945 a parade of allied armour damaged the circuit. Monza suffered the same fate as had Spa-Franchorchamps the previous year during the Battle of the Bulge when the caterpillar tracks of heavy tanks destroyed the track surface. Following this, Monza was used to store military vehicles and surplus equipment, the circuit falling further into disrepair.

Then Barbieri was spotted walking back to the pits from South Curve. It transpired that disaster had struck on the first lap. Campari had passed Borzacchini for the lead, but lost control on the oilslick. One of Campari's wheels had hooked the edge of the banking, forcing the car off the track after about 100 metres. It flipped over, crushing 'Negher' to death. Behind the leader, havoc, with drivers trying to avoid further accidents. Castelbarco's and Barbieri's cars both rolled, fortunately neither driver suffering serious injury. Borzacchini was not as lucky; his

Wolfgang von Trips rounds the banking in a Ferrari Dino 246P in 1960. Just a year later the German count lay dead by the side of the road course ...

Juan Manuel Fangio leads Mercedes team-mate Stirling Moss (both in the streamlined W196s) off the road course as an open wheeler exits the banking.

Restoration of the circuit took two months in 1948, and was undertaken by the Milan Automobile Club. Subsequently, the circuit that was used for racing was the 6.3km road course and not the combined version which included the high speed circuit.

In 1955 the high speed circuit was rebuilt, roughly following the 1922 plan but with much steeper banking. The new pista d'alta velocita (high speed track), had twin super-elevated curves with a 320 degree radius, and a progressive gradient up to 80 per cent at the top – designed to handle speeds of up to 285kph (177mph). The new circuit length equalled 4.250km (2.64 miles). Other improvements included new electronic scoreboards that followed the race; new offices, and a press pavilion. The new combined course hosted the 1955, 1956, 1960 and 1961 Italian rounds of the Formula One World Championship. It also played host to a fictional 1966 race in the film *Grand Prix*, Yves Montard's character, Jean Pierre Sarti, losing his life on the banking as his Ferrari launched from the top of the Southern Curve.

The high speed course hosted two very special events in 1957 and '58 – the 'Monzanapolis' 500 mile events. These 'two world' races pitched the American Indianapolis racers against the established stars of the European motor racing circus. The first race in 1957 entailed ten of the best from the US taking on ten of the best Europeans, both sides using regular machinery. However, on the run-up to the event a number of problems beset the European entry. *Autosport* magazine covered the race and its associated problems, most of which concerned safety.

"Despite all the head shaking, and refusal by certain European drivers to take part in the 500 mile race of Monza, the event went off without a single accident. It was a wonderful spectacle; the deep-throated roar of the Indianapolis cars evoking memories of prewar racing between Mercedes-Benz and Auto Union. Much nonsense has been talked about the perils of high speed track racing, but certain Scottish gentlemen with vast motor racing experience, and three courageous drivers made a certain Grand Prix coterie look a trifle silly.

"That curious organisation UPPI declared it would be suicide to race on the Monza banked circuit; tyres would fly off and there would be terrible crashes. And what happened? Excited spectators saw cars passing each other at over 180mph (290kph), lap speeds averaging 175mph (281kph), and a race average of over 160mph (257kph), all on a blazing hot day with temperatures of around 104 degrees F (40 degrees C). Yet there was not a single tyre failure, in fact, the tyres on the Jaguars were scarcely worn despite high lap speeds".

In the end there were just three entries from Europe, all from the Ecurie Ecosse Jaguar team. Three European sports cars against ten purpose-built American racers; it was the fastest race ever run in Europe, and even the American participants had never raced at such high speed. Their cars' rigid suspension set-up took a pounding on Monza's rough banking, the stress transmitting to other parts of the cars, causing chassis failure and resulting in retirement – as did split fuel tanks.

A pair of Porsches slipsteam past the pits toward the banking. The huge scoreboard is better than those found at most circuits today.

Three cars take to South Curve.

In 1966 the World Sportscar Championship took to the Monza banking. Pictured here is the beautiful Ferrari Dino 206S of Lorenzo Bandini and Ludovico Scarfiotti.

Nevertheless, the 13 car event was deemed a success and the Americans vowed to return, hopefully to face stronger opposition from the Europeans. And they did. The 1958 event became the world's fastest race to date when Jim Rathmann in his Zink Leader averaged 166.73mph (268.3kph) throughout the event, thus beating Hermann Lang's record set at AVUS by over 4mph (6.43kph). This time the European racing scene had put up a decent entry, featuring Mike Hawthorn, Luigi Musso, and Phil Hill who was driving a new 4.2 litre Ferrari; Harry Schell in a modified 1952 Ferrari; Stirling Moss in a 4.2 Maserati badged as the Eldorado-Italia, and Juan Manuel Fangio drove the Dean Van Lines Special. Two Ecurie Ecosse Jaguar D-types were also on the entry list driven by Masten Gregory and Ivor Bueb, along with a Jack Fairman-driven Lister Jaguar.

There was some doubt that the event would actually run because of the weather; as *Autosport* reported:

"Things looked fairly bleak in mid week, with a continuous downpour of rain which prevented any practice until Friday afternoon. Then the weather changed for the better and the organisers began to breathe freely. Postponement of the race would have entailed heavy financial loss, and the probability that European drivers would be unable to compete owing to commitments elsewhere".

The safety of the high speed course was commented on by Bob Veith, after his steering column came adrift, no doubt due to the rough nature of the banking surface. The Bob Estes special made it safely back to the pits. Veith remarked:

"Sure is a safe track; If that'd happened at Indy I'd have been through a wall!". Stirling Moss' special hit the wall due to a similar problem, but also escaped without major damage; the *Daily Express* newspaper ran a front page photograph of the accident.

The banked circuit saw occasional use during the 1960s and the Monzanapolis events were repeated. The last time a real Grand Prix ran on the banking was in 1961, an event most remembered for the horrific accident that claimed the lives of Ferrari driver Wolfgang von Trips and a number of spectators.

Use of both the banked circuit and combined course continued for a number of years, though the high speed bowl was stymied by chicanes intended to reduce the speed at which cars took the two curves. Eventually the banking fell out of use, the odd non-competitive nostalgia run being the only dedicated events. The banked course also hosted stages of the Monza rally, with extra chicanes added along the length of the track.

... and now

Today, the banked course is a haunting curiosity, which sweeps away from the modern Grand Prix circuit, an uncomfortable reminder of a bygone era, completely at odds with the ultra safe and clinical world of Formula One in its current guise. The Armco barriers which run around the top of the banked North and South Curves rust gently in the summer sun. In places painted-on sponsorship details crumble away to reveal more corroded steelwork. The start of the Southern Banking, which witnessed the blackest moments of Black Sunday, now hosts grandstands which overlook the first chicane on a modernised Monza road course.

Further round the curve the track crosses the road course on the approach to the Ascari chicane. In the mid-1990s someone made obvious their enthusiasm for their favourite Grand Prix racer by painting the driver's name on the banking, so now every time the leader passes under the banking, television cameras pick out the christian name of the 1996 Formula One world champion, Damon Hill.

The trees to the side of the track have encroached, and their rustling leaves seem to whisper the names of the great aces who once raced around this cauldron of speed. The straight linking South Curve to North is little used, save as a car park at major meetings on the road course. The surface, however, has been maintained, and is used by the FIA and Ferrari to test tyres and track surfaces, and to simulate wet weather conditions. Ferrari test drivers must be sorely tempted to keep their cars accelerating onto the banking at full tilt, the ever-present though faded yellow lines dancing away in the distance.

Monza's banked circuit should be but a memory, but it remains to tantalize racers and render spectators awestruck. It has seen off threats of destruction, yet it has no future. The Curva di Sopraelevata is the past – a ghost; was it ever real?

REIMS

The start of the 1939 French Grand Prix. A German benefit, Tazio Nuvolari leads his Auto Union team-mate Hermann Muller. The Auto Union D-types are out in front of the long Mercedes Benz racers.

The village of Gueux is a quiet, delicate little place. Between a pond in the centre of the village and the front of the church the name of the village is spelt out in a topiary bush. This gentle corner of France in the heart of the Champagne province couldn't be nicer if it tried.

However, about a kilometre to the west of the village there's a dark brooding presence keeping watch over the main road into the village. Faded advertising for local champagne houses peels away as unconcerned motorists sweep past, a few, perhaps, wondering what these deserted grandstands await.

It was once one of the world's great circuits, hosting world championship Grands Prix and top level sportscar races. The track was fast, very fast, made up of public roads on the edge of the village. A track on which both the Silver Arrows and Sharknose Ferraris ran now lies rotting and abandoned. The Circuit de Gueux – more often known as simply Reims or Reims-Gueux – stands as a reminder of those halcyon days of Formula One motor racing; of Ferrari, of Lotus, and many other great names which made this stretch of Tarmac the hallowed ground it is. Many millions of motor racing fans worldwide regard the place with the same reverence as that reserved for other great circuits, such as the full Spa-Francorchamps, the Nürburgring Nordschleife, and even Monaco. Reims was a place where legends were made and myths created.

The track was host to the 1961 French Grand Prix, and the winner – Giancarlo Baghetti – was driving in his first world championship race, the first and only time a Formula One world championship round has been won by a newcomer. The car Baghetti drove was even more legendary: the 1961 Ferrari 156 Dino was a beautifully crafted, V6 powered machine with such eye-catching styling that it became known simply as 'the Sharknose', a name which sticks to this day.

On August 2, 1925 the Circuit de Gueux sprang into life for the first time, hosting a meeting for both cars and bikes. Winner of the main event, the inaugural Grand Prix de la Marne, was Pierre Clause driving a 2 litre Bignan at an average speed of 102kph (74.5mph). The following year the 12 heure de Gueux sports car race – which became a very popular fixture on the international motor racing tour – was run for the first time. During the race the sunrise was an additional problem for the already challenged

drivers, who were dazzled by it on the approach to Thillois. An unlikely solution was found in the shape of a giant velvet curtain which was hung across the escape road just beyond the corner!

These opening meetings were just reward for the man who had dreamed up this blast through champagne country, Raymond 'Toto' Roche. His great granddaughter by marriage, Mary Roche Whittington, now heads the Amis de Circuit de Gueux (ACG) which cares for the ruins.

The new track consisted of a roughly triangular course made up from public roads with a total length of 7.826km (4.862 miles), and was situated just outside the small village of Gueux. Most of the circuit ran through open country but, at one point, darted through the outskirts of the village. It was decided that the start line would be on the CD27, a fairly minor road that mainly served the village. From there the cars ran down into Gueux village itself and turned sharp right between the buildings

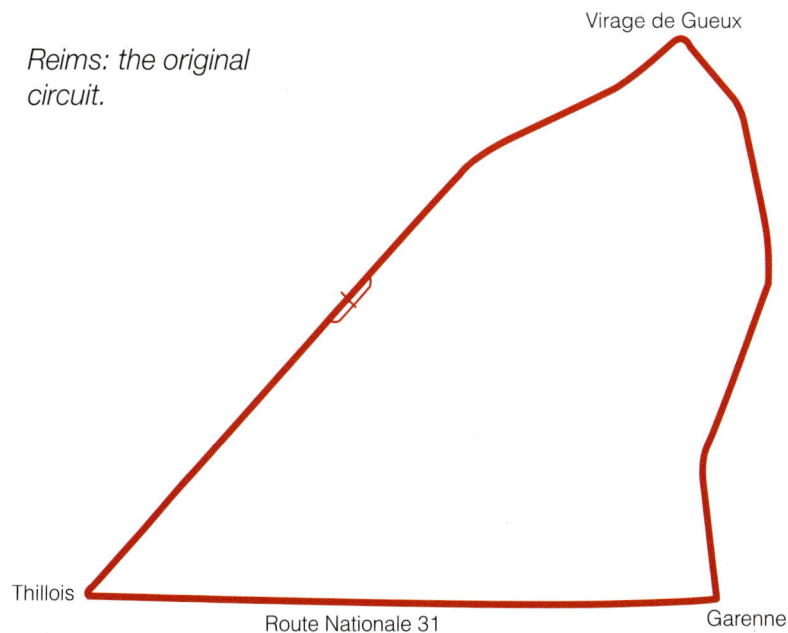

Reims: the original circuit.

45

Awaiting the start of the 1951 French Grand Prix, a packed field is headed by the Alfa Romeo 159s of Juan Manuel Fangio and Giuseppe Farina, along with the Ferrari 375 of Alberto Ascari.

and shops onto another minor road, the CD26, for a 2km (1.24 mile) gentle uphill run to La Garenne corner. Here, the track joined Route Nationale 31, a much more significant road which served Reims rather than outlying villages. The RN31 formed the main straight, sloping gently downhill to the right-handed Thillois Hairpin which led the circuit back onto the CD27, the finishing straight.

These first races were a success, and meetings continued to be held on the track at club and non-championship GP level until 1932 when the Circuit de Gueux hosted the Grand Prix de l'Automobile Club de France (ACF), effectively the French

Grand Prix. The circuit had truly arrived on the international scene, where it remained until closure decades later. The 'Flying Mantuan' Tazio Nuvolari won that first Grand Prix, driving the superb Vittorio Jano-designed Alfa Romeo P3. The race ran for a gruelling 461 miles (742km) at an average speed of 148.5kph (92.27mph); for a road course mainly consisting of long straights and hairpins it was clear that Reims was very fast indeed.

However, the following year the Grand Prix did not return to the Champagne circuit, instead heading to the Linas-Montlhéry circuit near Paris. It took six years for the GP to return, and when it did in 1938 it brought the Germans with it. A new timing

Piero Taruffi had a streamlined Maserati 250F for the 1956 French Grand Prix, such was the fast nature of the course.

hut had appeared at the beginning of the pit buildings, the Pavillon Andre Lambert, which remains to this day, in recently restored condition.

This was the prewar era of German supremacy in motorsport, when the awesomely advanced racers from Auto Union and Mercedes works teams went into action. The Stuttgart marque dominated proceedings in the 1938 race, with Manfred von Brauchtisch taking the spoils, then in 1939 it was Auto Union's turn and H. P. Muller was the winner. The 1938 Mercedes win was the first for the W125 Silver Arrow, one of the finest racing cars ever crafted, and now one of the most valuable.

It didn't take the circuit long to get back on its feet after the war years; perhaps its very nature, being made up of public roads, reduced the damage of enforced inactivity. The first post war meeting was run on August 3, 1947 from which the circuit quickly increased in significance to host the GP de l'ACF in 1948.

In the first few years of the track's return the Alfettas ruled the roost, and the 1.5 litre Alfa Romeo 158s were running quicker than anything had done before. The lap record rose to 119.99mph (193kph) in the 1951 race, a good 3mph (4.82kph) faster than the big prewar 3 litre Mercedes Silver Arrows ever acheived. However, the circuit was in need of major modification

47

Bretelle Sud

Courbe de Gueux

Annie Bousquet

Bretelle Nord

Hovette

Muizon

Thillois

Route Nationale 31

The wide open spaces of Reims. Here, in the 1958 Grand Prix, the Ferrari Dino 246 of Wolfgang von Trips leads the Vanwall of Tony Brooks.

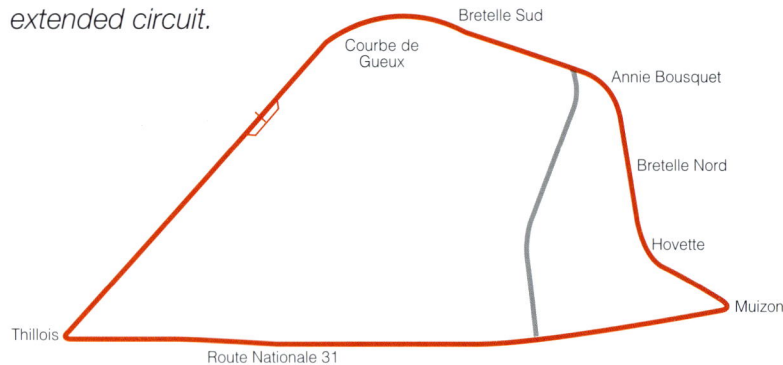

– because of, some say, a battle with Spa-Francorchamps for the title of fastest circuit in Europe. Work began in 1952 with the construction of a new southern section, Bretelle Sud, which linked the legs that ran to and from Gueux village in a large sweep before rejoining the old course at La Hovette corner. The circuit then continued as before up to La Garenne, the new overall length being 4.472 miles (7.196km).

A further change was made for the 1953 season when a new portion of track, named Bretelle Nord, was built linking the La Hovette section with the RN31 straight. This new course comprised a right-hand corner, followed by a downhill run ending in a left curve, with a new climb en route to connect with the RN31 at Muizon at a new, very tight corner. The new length came to 5.186 miles (8.345km), although a shorter 'test' circuit option was available using some of the 1952 circuit. Apart from a few minor changes in 1956 this was the circuit's definitive layout, the remains of which sit in the pretty Champagne countryside.

The first Grand Prix on the new configuration was to be a decisive one, a huge duel developing between Mike Hawthorn and the ever-performing Juan Manuel Fangio. However, this was superseded by entertainment of a different sort. Unusually, the 12 Heures de Gueux was run as part of the same meeting as the Grand Prix de l'ACF, and the race was to start at midnight and end at noon. The celebrations and pageantry began around 8pm with plenty of attractions; dancing girls galore, wrestling matches, acrobats, cabaret turns from Paris' Bal Tabearin and Moulin Rouge, nine dance bands for open air dancing, a mammoth firework display – and, of course – unlimited champagne. "Few of the great crowd there are likely to forget 'La Grande Nuit des Etoiles et du Champagne'", glowed *Autosport* the following week.

The Automobile Club de Champagne had made a real effort to equip the new circuit for night racing, going so far as to erect giant pylons to hold floodlights. At midnight the race started and, by the second lap, the 4.5 litre works Ferrari of Umberto Maglioli and Carini had taken a commanding lead, which it held until daybreak. Shortly before 5am it was seen running without lights,

contravening race regulations which state that all cars must run with lights ablaze until 5am. Then, the car went in for a pit stop and driver change just as the race director arrived in the Ferrari stall to witness the red car being serviced by more than the permitted number of mechanics. To compound matters further the car was then push-started – again, against the rules. The leading car was promptly disqualified and the somewhat vocal protests of the Ferrari team fell on deaf ears. The black flag was displayed to Maglioli as he passed the pits but he chose to ignore it. The crowd was riled by the officials' decision, vocalising this with boos, obscenities and catcalls. Display flowers were torn up and hurled onto the track, as the Italians continued to ignore their disqualification. Eventually, however, the car was forced out, leaving Stirling Moss and Peter Whitehead to win the race in their C-type Jaguar.

The 12 hours race was an appetiser for the main event, the Grand Prix. *Autosport* magazine was on hand to cover what it described as "THE RACE OF THE CENTURY". In one of the greatest motor races ever run, Mike Hawthorn saved the day for Scuderia Ferrari after being involved in a fantastic battle with Juan Manuel Fangio (Maserati) for more than half the 60 lap distance of the new Gueux circuit at Reims. *Autosport's* coverage went on to state that the two red cars flashed past the pits, absolutely neck-and-neck in the closing laps, at least ten times.

Before the flag had even dropped there was speculation about whether the Ferrari team – still disgusted after disqualification in the 12 hours race – would start. Rumours circulated that the team's cars would run only the minimum number of laps to fulfill contractual obligations. At the race start, however, four red cars with Prancing Horses painted on the side lined up on the grid ...

As the starter, Charles Faroux, unfurled the flag to start the race, the crowd again voiced its displeasure at the disqualification of Ferrari in the endurance race, boos and hisses emanating from the tribunes. The flag dropped and the race started, 'Pampas bull' Frolian Gonzalez blasting into the lead from the third row in a Maserati 250F, leaving front row drivers Fangio and Bonetto in shock as he surged away from them. By the time the 24 car field shrieked down through Garrenne an almighty scrap was developing.

Gonzalez was leading, followed by a tightly packed bunch consisting of Ascari, Villoresi, Fangio, Hawthorn, Bonetto, Marimon and Farina, with Bira hot on the heels of this bunch of red cars. At the end of lap two Gonzalez had pulled out a four second advantage and looked like increasing it even more. Behind him battle was raging for second position. *Autosport* takes up the story:

"With Gonzalez out in front, the fierce struggle behind never did let up for a moment. The Maserati did the first five laps at an average speed of over 112mph (180.24kph). Fangio began to close up on Farina, whilst Ascari, Hawthorn and Villoresi continually chopped and changed places - less than half a second separating all three."

After ten laps the leader was sevens seconds ahead, with the top drivers placed as follows: 1. Gonzalez (Maserati), 2. Hawthorn (Ferrari), 3. Ascari (Ferrari), 4. Villoresi (Ferrari), 5. Farina (Ferrari), 6. Fangio (Maserati). Gonzalez kept increasing his lead, and at 20 laps had an 18 second advantage with four Ferraris still battling it out. However, Fangio thought it about time he got in on the act and swept past Farina under the Dunlop Bridge, only to be retaken by Farina into Thillois. On lap 24 occurred a most extraordinary sight. After Gonzalez went through, Ascari, Villoresi, Hawthorn, Fangio, Farina and Marimon – all trying to pass each other – hurtled en masse past the tribunes. Even the Maserati and Ferrari pit staff were shaken; pity the poor team managers who had to convey positions to the drivers!

Then the manoeuvring began: Fangio was on the move, whistling past three cars to sit on Ascari's tail; Gonzalez signalled that he was coming into the pits for fuel, having begun the race on half full tanks. Fangio then aknowledged a mysterious code on his pit board. Gonzalez tore out of the pits having lost 28 seconds, and dropped to sixth place. The next lap a scrap for the lead began, with Fangio, Ascari and Hawthorn tearing around desperately trying to get in front. Ascari lost ground leaving Fangio and Hawthorn out in front, where *Autosport* takes up the story once more:

"The fight at the front continued unabated. Fangio and Hawthorn kept up their epic ding-dong, and the crowd all round the circuit was almost beserk with exitement. The Argentinian was bringing all his vast experience into play, but could make no impression on that cool, green-clad figure in the Ferrari. Everyone seemed to sense that Fangio had met another master of motor racing. This was certainly Mike Hawthorn's hour, and Enzo Ferrari must have blessed the day he signed up the Farnham flyer."

With five laps to go, Fangio came past the pits a wheel width ahead of Hawthorn, and round they went, chopping and changing. Four laps to go and Fangio weaved as Hawthorn tried to pass. Mike took to the grass momentarily in front of the new timing box, recovered, and the pair levelled as they disappeared under the Dunlop bridge.

The excitement was indescribable, with everyone on their feet. In the tribunes scores of field glasses were focused on Thillois. Up in the press tribune the Argentinian commentator was practically in a state of collapse after jabbering non-stop for over two-and-a-half hours, with barely a moment's breathing space! Three laps later Fangio and Hawthorn were again dead level past the timing box. Hard-headed journalists, veterans of dozens of Grand Prix events, lost their usual nonchalance and became madly excited onlookers. One gentleman even went so far as to tear up his notes, stand on his hat and, finally, fall over his desk!

The last lap: for the tenth time the leaders dead heated over the line. No-one will ever forget that finish, at Thillois Hawthorn edged ahead of his rival and held his slender lead all the way down the straight. Down came the flag with the Ferrari about 40 yards in front of the Maserati.

However, before everyone could let out their held breath there was another terrific thrill. Making a last minute bid, Gonzalez left Ascari standing out of Thillois, and tore down the straight, all but catching Fangio on the line. In this 'Race of the Century', just 7.6 seconds separated the first five cars.

Reims had become France's premier motor racing circuit (with the exception, perhaps, of Le circuit de la Sarthe at Le Mans). It played host to the French round of the Formula One World Championship on a regular basis; the Grand Prix taking only the occasional break to visit Rouen-les-Essarts and Clermont-Ferrand. The circuit also periodically hosted stages of the French and World Cycle Championships, the Tour de France

Graham Hill was one of many world champions who raced around the roads outside Gueux.

Auto, and various high profile motorcycle meetings. The decade between mid fifties and mid sixties was the circuit's golden era; the stands were always packed and everything went smoothly. But the days of pure road courses (as opposed to street circuits) were numbered for car racing, and today only a few remain in neutered form like Spa-Francorchamps and Le Mans. One of the reasons for this was clearly the safety aspect. Such a fast course based on public roads was bound to be dangerous, and the Circuit de Gueux claimed the lives of a number of competitors, amongst their number Luigi Musso, killed in an accident at Courbe de Gueux during the 1958 Grand Prix, which was also Juan Manuel Fangio's final Grand Prix. Enzo Ferrari commented on his driver's fate: "I have won at Reims but the price is too high. I have lost the only Italian driver who mattered".

The Grand Prix circus pitched its tent at Reims for the final time in 1966, heading the following year to the new Bugatti circuit at Le Mans. That final Grand Prix was run at some speed, too, Bandini turning in the fastest ever lap at Reims in practice at 2:07.8, 233.8kph (145.3mph) and Jack Brabham winning the race.

The circuit went into decline from this point, with the final 12 hours race – an annual fixture – occurring the following year. The 1968 race was scheduled and looked certain to take place until the riots which were sweeping the country at that time resulted in its cancellation. The following year was to be the final one for car racing; on June 29 the Formula Two circus arrived for what turned out to be the last ever meeting at Reims. Following the race a press release was issued about the future of the circuit:

"Modifications being studied to give the Reims circuit a layout conforming with current racing regulations will require inspections and alteration work taking several months. Consequently, the Automobile Club of Champagne, wishing to carry out alterations so that its races take place under the best conditions, has decided not to organize the Reims car race meeting in 1970, and instead offer starting positions to amateur racing drivers for 1971."

The work was never done for a number of reasons, one of which was that the proposed changes would simply be far too expensive. Widening of the pit straight to accommodate a proper pit lane and wall (Reims only ever had a Tarmac apron and pit counter) would have required the demolition and reconstruction of the pit and paddock complex – a major undertaking, especially as Clermont-Ferrand was pushing hard to become the regular host of the Grand Prix. Motorcycle racing did, however, continue at the circuit into the seventies, for a while at least. With the cars gone, though, a good proportion of support for racing dried up. Yves Compan won the last ever race at the Circuit de Gueux on 11 June, 1972, riding his 750cc Honda bike.

The organisers packed up their belongings and left the circuit, never to return. The pit and paddock stood empty and untouched until early 2004, apart from bored tourists doing a spot of exploring, and wanton vandalism, when the locals decided to begin restoration of the circuit buildings. In the winter of 2000 a road realignment scheme for Gueux meant annihilation of the Muizo-Thillois section, which was replaced by a new road; La Garenne was cut off by an overpass. The original road can be followed for a distance until, in the middle of a farmer's field, a small wooden cross – flowers by its side – marks the point at which it ends.

... and now

Today, the circuit has reverted to public road use. Nothing distinguishes it from any other French back road; nothing, that is, until you reach the old start/finish area which is like a snapshot of motor racing in the late 1960s. Imagine one of today's Grand Prix circuits – the new Nürburgring, maybe – abandoned and untouched for thiry-five years, and you might get an idea of just how atmospheric Reims is.

Pretty much everything remains – albeit suffering the effects of forty years of decay – bar a couple of buildings. Rising to the

Pit fever during the 12 hours race: just a few years later the circuit was abandoned. (Courtesy LAT)

left are the two huge tribunes; facing them across the road is the pit and paddock complex. Once packed full of roaring crowds, they now sit quietly by the roadside in the deafening silence.

There is so much to see: exploration under the two main grandstands reveals ticket offices and restaurants; the rear of the stands, like every other surface in the area, are covered in faded, flaking and forgotten adverts for BP, Esso, L'Equipe and Veedol, amongst others. Selling their wares to an audience no longer buying.

A sign naming the stand 'Tribune Raymond Sommer' is being repainted with great care by a member of the ACG; above him on the pleated and curving roof of the stand a Dunlop logo gradually fades into memory.

Beyond the large main two tribunes lie a pair of smaller open stands, overgrown with blackberry bushes. Arches and pillars in the field behind the stands are vaguely reminiscent of the megaliths at Stonehenge in the south west of England, but rather than ancient ceremonial features, these are all that remain of the spectator entrance gates, a monument to the past.

On the far side of the road there is much more: the main pit building consisting of a line of pit boxes alongside the apron; the paddock complex and associated structures. About halfway up the line of pit boxes towers a building used as a restaurant area. Inside the pit boxes at the far end are the remains of some refuelling equipment, now rusting and open to the elements. The tower and tank that kept them full of fuel lie off to the left, rusting gently in the afternoon sun. Above the pit boxes are more faded avertisements; every wall has faded marking of some kind.

Exploring the back of the pit building turns up the overgrown paddock – and the paddocks main access point, a large, two-lane tunnel. It shows some signs of flooding but otherwise appears in very good condition. Somewhat worse for wear, and mostly bricked up, is the foot tunnel, the steps on the paddock side buried in rubble, though clearer on the tribune side.

Many of the walls around the complex are adorned with graffiti, which has damaged the period painted walls and contributed to the general air of abandonment.

When the Roman empire turned its back on Britain it left behind many abandoned structures, and the remains that sit by the Route Nationale 31 are evocative of these, former glory fading in the late summer evening sunshine, as nature slowly reclaims these edifices. Just as the Roman gladiators played out life and death scenarios in the arena, here, horses were replaced by machines, and shield and armour by helmet and goggles. Gone but not quite forgotten, the world has simply moved on, leaving behind a ruined temple to the great gods of speed.

Continuing, the track itself is mostly intact apart from the previously mentioned roundabout at the entry of the Courbe de Gueux, and another at the remnants of Thillois Hairpin, both of which form part of the road improvements of 2000. Since closure of the circuit the Route Nationale 31 has been widened and is now a busy dual carriageway.

The pre-1952 circuit is easily driven today, and the buildings around the Virage de Gueux appear little changed. It's doubtful that the village of Gueux has changed much either; one local told me that a building next to the circuit still bore the scar from a wound inflicted by a German racer in the 1930s. The building in question certainly does have a scrape in the right spot but how it really came to be can only be guessed at ...

A group of local enthusiasts, known as Amis de Circuit de Gueux (ACG) are trying, slowly, to restore parts of the track. Minimal funding and only voluntary work makes progress difficult but 'les amis' have succeeded in restoring the appearance of the timing pavillion (Pavillon Andre Lambert). The club also safeguards the track's history, collecting every shred of media output connected to the circuit. Recently, the organisation faced the challenge of a large detachment of gypsies, or travellers, setting up camp in the old paddock. The intruders boarded up the freshly painted pavillion to hold a wedding party. Happily, the travellers took note of the ACG's pleas and the 'Respect the site' stencils dotted about the place, the only damage being a small amount of graffiti.

Word has it that the buildings are threatened with demolition, but it's doubtful that this will ever happen. Local residents are proud of their motor racing heritage to the extent that many would like to see motor racing return. Given the amount of money the champagne companies turn over it would not be a surprise if they stumped up the funds to return les Circuit de Gueux to action, still using the old pits and paddock: what an event that would be!

MEMOIRE DES PILOTES
RESPECT DU SITE

PAVILLON
Andre LAMBERT

BP

TRIBUNE RAYMOND SOMMER
ESSO
toujours
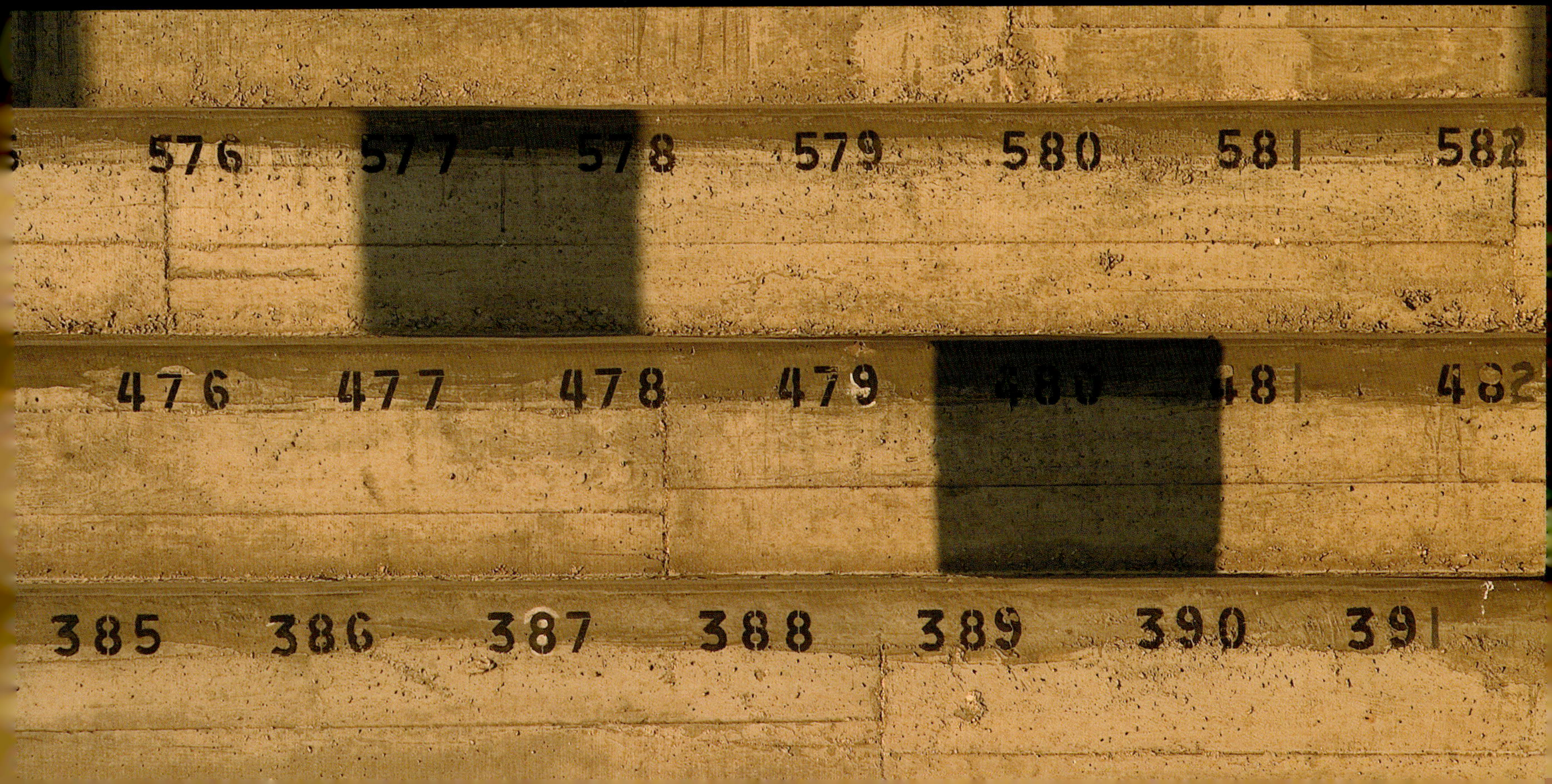
576 577 578 579 580 581 582
476 477 478 479 480 481 482
385 386 387 388 389 390 391

NÜRBURGRING SÜDSCHLEIFE

Nürburgring circuit.

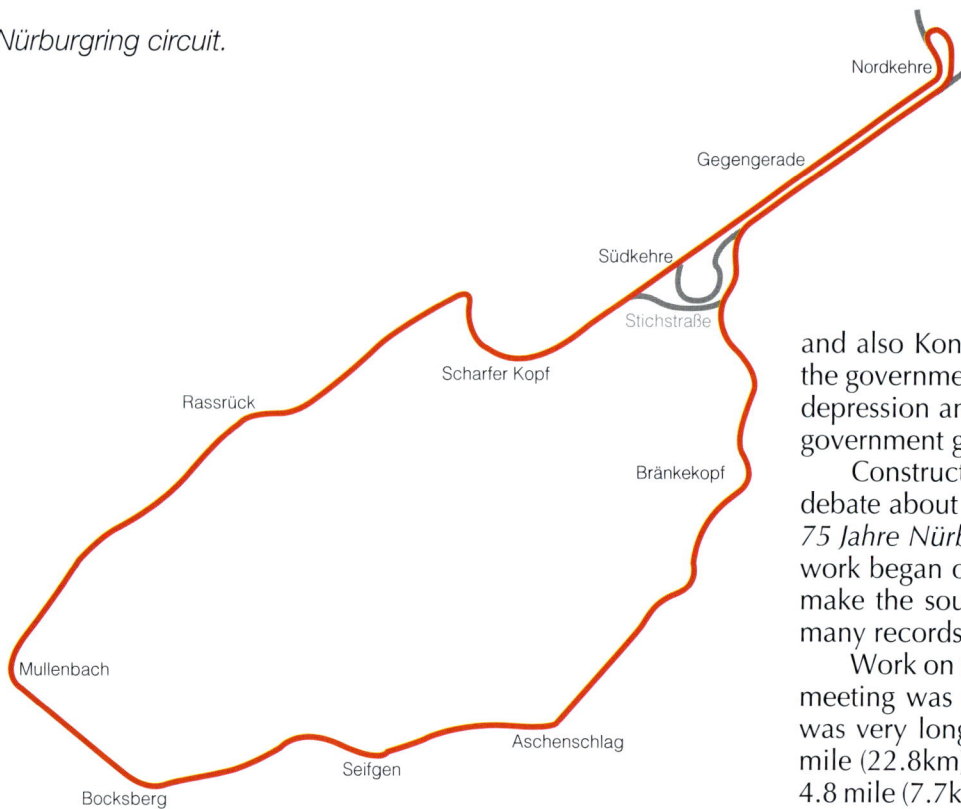

From the early days drivers had a fear of the track; some claimed it to be haunted by ancient spirits, which would emerge from between the trees at the side of the track and force a car off the track at speed. Without doubt a number of strange and inexplicable crashes occurred on the Südschleife, and in 1935 drivers refused point-blank to race on it during the Grand Prix. It does seem far-fetched, however, to claim that ghosts were responsible for the accidents. Whatever the reason, the track was little used throughout its existence, compared with the Nordschleife part of the track at least.

Germany, home nation of the car, has always enjoyed success when it comes to motorised sport. In 1907 the popularity of competition motoring led to the introduction of the Kaiserpreis series of races. Perhaps as a result of Brooklands, a permanent testing venue for German manufacturers was mooted, and suggested locations included an area in the Eifel mountains, amongst others. However, no conclusion had been drawn by the time Europe descended into bloody war.

It wasn't until 1921 that the idea resurfaced. AVUS (Automobil Verkehrs-Ubungstrasse) – a circuit made up of autobahn just outside Berlin – was used for racing, then, in 1925, Dr Otto Creuz, a member of the Eifel district council, came up with the idea of the Nürburgring and submitted it in April 1925. He gained the support of ADAC, the German motorsports governing body,

and also Konrad Adenauer, mayor of Cologne, who persuaded the government to support the idea. The region was in economic depression and the benefits of a dedicated track were clear: the government granted the project 14.1 million Reichsmarks.

Construction began on 27 September, 1925. There's some debate about precisely where work first started but, in his book, *75 Jahre Nürburgring*, Michael Behrndt claims that construction work began on the Südschleife or southern section. This would make the southern loop the oldest part of the 'ring. However, many records were lost during the Second World War.

Work on the circuit was completed in 1927 and the opening meeting was run on 18/19 June over the full circuit. The track was very long, and could also be split in two: the longer 14.2 mile (22.8km) Nordschleife for international races and the short 4.8 mile (7.7km) Südschleife designed for club racing and testing. Combining the two tracks made the Gasamstrecke heavyweight of the circuit world at 17.5 miles (28.265km).

During the track's first few years of existence, the two circuits were combined most of the time and races were run over the full 28km (19 miles). The first time the shorter track was used was during the Eifelrennen in May 1928 when the final race of the day saw bikes and cars competing together on the same track – a rare occurrence. A couple of weeks later during a 357km (220 miles) race a new track record was established; 5m 00.06 was now the mark to beat.

Those with an interest in motor racing know of the Nordschleife's daunting reputation, a track that has claimed the lives of many speed merchants over the years, and still does on a regular basis. The 'ring's most famous incident didn't actually involve any fatalities, though it very nearly claimed the life of the reigning Formula One World Champion; this was, of course, Nike Lauda's horrific fiery smash during the German Grand Prix in 1976. That accident occurred near the most northerly point of the northern loop.

However, few know very much about the equally challenging but shorter circuit a few kilometres to the south. The circuit used the same start and finish stretch as the Nordschleife, a 500 metre (1640ft) long straight of 20 metres' (65ft) width. The course ran down to the first corner where it separated from the Nordschleife at Südkehre, an almost ninety degree left-hand turn. Now on

Hans Hermann in his Porsche 718/2, car 14.

the Südschleife cars proceeded out of the turn and plunged downhill underneath a road bridge. After the bridge the track swept down into a valley, through a snake of left- and right-hand curves, which led into the Brankekopf section of track, a tricky, writhing group of turns that smoothed into a short straight. Next up was the fast right-hander, Aschenschlag, followed by a short straight and slight left kink. Emerging from the kink after Aschenschlag, racers were immediately presented with Seifgen, a right-left combination, the left opening out gradually into a fast and straight-ish section that rushed towards the Blocksberg kink. Blocksberg – a fast right-hander that claimed the life of biker Dickie Dale in 1961 during the Eifelrennen event – is the southern extremity of the Nürburgring, some 7.5km (4.6 miles) from Bergwerk corner.

After Blocksberg the course ran right round to the outskirts of the village of Mullenbach; the ninety degree right-hand corner here at the course's lowest point bears the village's name. After Mullenbach the track began to climb back uphill into Rassruck, a fast climb through the forest. At the climb's summit lies one of the tightest turns – almost a hairpin – on the Südschleife, Scharfer-Kopf. The right-hander immediately flows back into a left sweep, opening into a long straight and rejoining the Nordschleife at Gegengerade running parallel to the start/finish line. The

Südschleife again splits from the northern loop at Nordkehre, a very wide left-hander that spat cars into the Betonkehre (so named as it was made out of 'beton', the German word for concrete), a right-hand turn that brought cars round onto the start/finish straight to complete a 7.747km (4.8 mile) lap.

The Südschleife was always the overlooked part of the ring, used far less than the Nordschleife. There are a number of reasons for this, ghosts aside. It was never intended that the southern loop should hold big races or international events but, by the 1930s, such events had become a matter of prestige. Germany was on a mission to prove its greatness, and German cars swept the board in every major race. The Nordschleife was the greatest track of all; a German win in the greatest car on the greatest track was a major boost for Germany. The daunting northern loop's prominence grew and crowds of over 200,000 attended the German Grand Prix.

Südschleife was not entirely forgotten; although races were run only infrequently, it was a popular testing facility, and well maintained. A link section of track was built to allow Nordschleife and Südschleife to be used at the same time. Stichstrasse ran from near the pedestrian bridge at the 6km (3.72 mile) post to just after the bridge at Südkehre. Narrow, single track and quite bumpy, this tree-lined section was never used for official racing purposes.

A field of sports and saloon racers appears from the ethereal mist which often hung over the circuit.

Racing at the Nürburgring ceased in late 1939 as Germany had other things to occupy it. When American forces arrived in Mullenbach in March of 1945, their commander ordered a group of tanks up the Südschleife toward the Schafer-Kopf, whilst another group headed up the track in the wrong direction toward the start/finish straight. This area and the Gegengerade section were used as HQ by the allied forces.

The track was badly damaged by the tanks, and years of neglect from 1939 took their toll. With help from the French government the Südschleife was rebuilt in 1947, commencing with the start/finish line in May that year. There were few alterations; a new surface and slight banking on some turns. The southern loop's inaugural event was a bike race in August, to which some 80,000 fans paid the 5 Deutschmark admission fee. 9 races were held, riders wearing different colour helmets to show in which class they were competing. The northern loop was not completely repaired until 1949.

From 1950 the Südschleife was used on a regular basis, and continued to be so throughout the next decade. In 1953 Formula 3 cars descended upon the southern loop, and Heinz Weeke set the fastest lap of the 10 lap race, his time of 4m 39 seconds equating to an average speed of 100kph (62mph.

Some minor circuit changes were made during the 1950s. In 1955 the Gengengerade was widened to 12 metres (39ft) and resurfaced in Tarmac, and in 1957 the entire start and finish area – with the exception of Betonkehre – was re-covered in Tarmac. After this had been done, the Südschleife began to run a few more high profile events. The annual Eifelrennen meeting returned to the southern loop during the fifties, Wolfgang von Trips winning the '59 race in his Fiat, and setting the fastest lap in 3m 40.1.

What should have been the Südschleife's greatest day came on August 1, 1960. The XXII Grosser Pries von Deutschland (German Grand Prix) was run on the southern loop. The race was actually run to Formula 2 regulations but still attracted some big names; Jo Bonnier, von Trips, Graham Hill, Hans Hermann and Edgar Barth lined up in Porsche 718/2s, and pitched against them was the Lotus 18 pairing of Innes Ireland and Dan Gurney, and a huge gaggle of Coopers, whose drivers included Jack Brabham, Bruce McLaren and Jo Schlesser, amongst others.

However, the malevolent spirits of the woods around the Südschleife were up to no good as spectator turn out was poor, and the weather was terrible. Fog gave way to torrential rain, and so much water fell from the leaden sky that Mullenbach Corner flooded deeply and had to be pumped dry by the local fire brigade. Finally, the circuit was deemed as ready as it ever would be, and the race was started.

Autosport magazine reported on the event in its 5 August issue: "Thick fog and an almost continuous downpour of rain set the scene for the German Grand Prix, held on Sunday for Formula 2 cars as a Constructor's Championship event on the shorter Südschleife or south circuit at the Nürburgring. Conditions were at their worst – the weather, it was generally agreed, was even more unpleasant than at this year's 1000kms sports car race at the circuit – and that went on record as the worst ever for the Eifel.

"The race was a real victory for Porsche. With the non-appearance of Ferrari after a disagreement with the Automobile Club von Deutschland, the only challenge came from world champion Jack Brabham, who performed miracles with an outclassed 'old' type Cooper to take third place. But first, second, fourth, fifth and sixth places went to the German marque, Joakim Bonnier scoring the outright win and crossing the line just over a second ahead of Wolfgang von Trips. Jack Brabham's third place – the result of a strategy worked out the night before – means that Cooper and Porsche share the lead in the Formula 2 Constructor's Championship with 26 points each."

The full report ran to four pages, continuing with a description of the southern loop, and mentioning the quality of surface in the Betonkehre and Nordkehre sections.

"The hairpin is surfaced with concrete slabs, between which are enormous cracks, and it is understood that the surface is that which was laid down in 1927!"

The small track reached its peak following the Grand Prix and throughout the 1960s with a number of Formula 2 and 3 races taking place. The staple pair of annual Südschleife events during that period were the Eifelrennen in April and the Eifelpokal Rennen in September.

During the early sixties the dangers of the sport were brought home when two competitors were killed during the

Car 25; Tony Marsh's Cooper T45.

1960 Eifelrennen, and then in 1961 the Eifelpokal Rennen was cancelled because Germany's best racer, Count Wolfgang von Trips, was killed in his Ferrari at Monza during the Italian Grand Prix a few weeks earlier. From 1962, in memory of the late hero, the Eifel Pokal Rennen was renamed the International Eifel Rennen Graf Trips Gedachtnis-Rennen. Lap speed was increasing, too; during the 1962 Eifelrennen Kurt Ahrens Jr bullied his Lotus 22 around the track in 3m 12.2.

Cars 4 and 23, the Cooper T51s of Oliver Gendebien and Lucien Bianchi, race out of the forest.

A new event debuted at the Nürburgring in 1966. The Marathon de la Route was an 84 hour monster run on the Gesamtstrecke, and a new formula, Vee. In 1968 the southern loop held a very big meeting, the annual Eifel Rennen attracted 200,000 people over two days. On the bill was a well attended formula two race and also the Grand Prix for motorcycles. One of the races during that event was stopped 7 laps early when smoke from a forest fire blanketed a section of the track, making racing impossible.

The circuit was on the wane at the end of that decade, however, and the last time the combined Gesamtstrecke circuit

was used for a major event was in 1970 for the Marathon de la Route. Motor racing technology was advancing rapidly; during a race for group 5, 6 and 7 cars Helmut Kelleners pedalled his March-Chevrolet 707 around in the record time of 2m 38.6, at an average speed of 108mph (173kph). The Südschleife was becoming fast and dangerous, like the Nordschleife.

The end was nigh and the last major meeting on the Südschleife was during the Mayener Rundstreckenrennen for F3 cars in October 1971. Safety in the sport was becoming paramount: the only reason a 300km (186.4 mile) F3 race was run on the southern loop in April was that the northern loop was undergoing major work to improve this aspect. The Südschleife was a fast and twisting track with no run-off to speak of, no escape roads, poor access for emergency vehicles, and almost no protection for spectators. Some may also have remembered it was claimed that something lurked amongst the trees ...

It seems that poor access and poor safety provision killed the track, but it was the size of the venue that delivered the fatal blow. The Nordschleife offered the huge volume of spectators lots of free movement, which the smaller track simply couldn't. Throughout its existence the Südschleife had always played second fiddle to its much larger neighbour. Unpopular with the drivers, it was never long for this world. In 1975 the track was finally closed to the tourist drivers who could pay a fee to drive on the track, much like the system that operates today on the Nordschleife. It was promptly abandoned and forgotten, apart from being used as a car park on occasion for big events hosted on the Nordschleife. During its fully active life from 1927 to 1971 the Nürburgring Südschleife claimed the lives of 19 drivers, some racers, some tourists; despite this, the circuit was soon forgotten.

The Nürburgring GmbH had been investigating a new, safer circuit during the 1970s with a variety of suggested layouts, but none was developed. Then Lauda's horrific accident during the 1976 Grand Prix brought matters came to a head. The 'ring had lost the German GP, a new track was needed. Eyes turned to the start/finish area and the land to the south, the Südschleife. In 1981 the first stone was laid on the new Nürburgring, the Grand Prix Strecke, a 4.5km (2.79 mile) circuit with Formula One participation firmly in its sights. The old start/finish area was torn up in 1982 and other sections of the Südschleife were destroyed, though some were converted to public road.

... and now

Today, what's left of the circuit gives many hints to what must have been an incredible track to race on. From just before Brankekopf down to Blocksberg the public road follows the course of the Südschleife. Of the run down to Mullenbach there is very little sign, just a small path running where the track once did. The section from Rassruck up to Scharfer-Kopf is still much as it was in 1975 – abandoned – apart from being used on occasion as part of a rally stage, where drivers are often heard referring to Scharfer-Kopf as 'Laubkurve', due to the often leaf-covered surface. (Laub is German for leaves.)

The ever-present fog meanders through the forest that surrounds the track, thin wisps seeming to reach out from between the trees; it's no wonder that some thought this place was haunted! Climbing up the hill from Mullenbach the old track runs roughly parallel to a new section of road. The atmosphere is similar to that of an abandoned church, unsure if the once holy ground is still consecrated. From the ditches to the side of

the Tarmac spring a line of younger trees, grown up since the circuit closed, and creating a barrier between the forest and the forgotten track. The backdrop is one of sheer beauty, the quiet village heralding a wider view across the Eifel mountains. The Nürburging is the most visually dramatic circuit in the world and the sheer scale of it has to be seen to be believed.

At the summit of the rise from Mullenbach is a steeply banked curve leading into Scharfer-Kopf and arrival back in civilization. Nordschleife maintenance lorries rumble past, and here the Südschleife vanishes, the run into start und ziel schliefe, the two parallel straights once linked by Betonkurve that hosted the pits, is simply no more. Now the area is dominated by the modern Grand Prix circuit spectator banks and tribunes rising up where the cars once raced.

There is no sign of the circuit until the start of the downhill section back towards Mullenbach village, now accessed from the wide main road that runs behind the pits. The Südschleife here is now known as the K72. The road ghosts the southern loop of the Nürburgring exactly through its downhill section, though there's little to differentiate it from any other of the twisting roads in the area, apart, that is, from its foreboding atmosphere. Here, the trees rise high, reaching for the sky through the shifting mists of the Eifel. A small concrete post that was once part of the course furniture, holding a telephone to summon help in the event of an accident, is all that remains. Apart from memories.

The road splits away from the old circuit just before Blocksberg corner, and you are drawn into the village. At Gasthaus Gilles the Ferrari-obsessed owner happily reminisces about the last days of the circuit's life – when villagers took part in what they call 'hobby races' on the abandoned track. "One big accident, and Nürburgring GmbH said …", the restaurateur, lost for English, gestures to show that the circuit owners prevented any more activity on the Südschleife because of safety concerns.

The Nürburgring museum ignores the Südschleife, as do most track maps – as, in fact, do most people. To many it's just the name of a street on the edge of Mullenbach. In years to come the villagers will forget, too, and the circuits will once again belong to the forest and its spirits ..

Adenau
9 km

Nürburg

CRYSTAL PALACE

Crystal Palace has been described as the crazy golf of motor racing. Via a number of different track layouts the circuit wound its way between fishing lakes, alongside a maze, past a zoo, and a group of life-size dinosaur models. The Palace was renowned as an international venue and played host to a number of great names from the continent: lap record holders included Hulme, Ickx, Beltoise, Rindt, Peterson and Fittipaldi, amongst many others. Despite this status the Formula One world championship was never held at Crystal Palace. Efforts are now being made to run a Grand Prix in London, but few remember that, years ago, the city had its own purpose-built race circuit.

Crystal Palace is one of motorsport's oldest venues. The start of competitive motoring at Crystal Palace predates the opening of Shelsley Walsh and Brooklands. With that in mind, could Crystal Palace claim to be the birthplace of British motorsport, a title currently held by Brooklands and Bexhill upon Sea?

Whilst researching this book I kept on discovering earlier and earlier events and meetings, so I'm by no means certain that the following account is of the first meeting, though it was certainly one of the first. Crystal Palace must have a legitimate claim as the oldest motorsport venue in Britain, and possibly the longest history – 101 years – of all venues. The track experienced periods of activity from 1899 right up until 2000, but as you will discover later in the book, its history may extend even further ...

The early days of British motoring were filled with many jolly events run by enthusiasts. Runs and reliability trials were the order of the day – as were major city-to-city races. However, our attention is drawn to one particular event. The year 1899; a Saturday in early May, and the venue was the bank of the River Thames. The law which compelled all motorists to be preceded by a man on foot waving a red flag had been repealed just a few years earlier, and the pioneers of motoring were beginning

1899 was the first year that Crystal Palace was used for motorsport, with cars competing in a variety of events including closed course circuit racing on the banked oval cycle racing track. (Courtesy LAT)

to explore the possibilities of motorised sport – in a very civil manner, of course. On May 6th that year, the Motor Car Club had organised a meet of cars with some competition activity on the track at the Crystal Palace. The cars were to meet at Westminster Bridge at noon and then proceed to the park in convoy. Their route was through Brixton, Streatham, and along Crystal Palace Parade before entering the park at 'Rockhills'.

There was some confusion about exactly when the convoy would depart. *Autocar* followed the event in its May 13th issue of the same year:

"No sort of order appeared to have been arranged and no-one seemed to be in charge of the gathering, so it was not surprising when at about 12.15 it was suddenly discovered that the front portion of the assemblage had disappeared, apparently without instruction to those behind, who were complacently awaiting permission to go. Then, one after the other, as the fancy moved him, each drew out and the thousand or so spectators who had turned out dispersed as the last car wound its way over the bridge".

Along the route a number of cars joined the now disjointed convoy, including some notable entries. C. S. Rolls was present in a new Panhard racer, there was an electric car known as a Clift, and Daimler Wagonette driven by Mr W. M. Morris to name but three entries. Upon arrival at the park the forty or so vehicles lined up on each side of the parade ground. (The period photos suggest that this was on the Italianate terraces above the aptly named Terrace Straight.) Most vehicles remained stationary to allow those who had gathered to admire them, but a few enthusiastic riders "... freely and rapidly patrolled the pathways ..." as the *Autocar* journalist put it.

A series of 'control tests' had been arranged and were the afternoon's main event. The format of these tests does not seem too dissimilar to a modern day speed event. A two-mile course (the exact layout of which seems to have been lost over time) had been laid out, and the aim was to complete the course in the shortest possible time. However, it wasn't as simple as it sounds, as the course was sinuous with quite a few gradient changes. To make matters worse for these very early motor cars and motorcycles, at 6 points around the course the competitor was obliged to stop between two flags placed about seven metres apart. A car or motorcycle which failed to stop between these flags faced disqualification.

The competitive part of the event was due to start at 2pm, but due to lack of organisation the first motorcycle set off forty minutes late, followed by another six competitors. Word soon reached the start line that only two had finished the course, and a fair distance apart at that. The two finishers were Richardson and Jarrott, but as for the other four starters little was known. A delegation was sent to investigate, including the *Autocar* journalist, who commented: "From then on it was extremely difficult to elicit any information from the judging line as to what test was really going on, and we therefore found our way to stopping points 2 and 3, the first at the bottom of a long gentle sloping downgrade, and the second at the end of an abrupt descent of about one in eight, or thereabouts, with an acute angled turn immediately following.

"Here we found that both controlling officials in charge had a small pile of trophies in the shape of numbers detached from competing cars which had failed to pull up in the required distance, and we understand that when these disqualifications were made, matters were for a time lively, especially with the motorcyclists".

Different approaches to this tricky section were tried by riders and drivers, some cars creeping very slowly down the hill, others going for it at breakneck speed, then slamming on the brakes to jerk to a halt. It must have been exiting to see – the *Autocar* report singles out C. S. Rolls in particular as being one of the most 'dashing'.

However, for all the carrying on and bouts of 'dashing' and/or 'lively' behaviour, no accidents were reported; amazing, considering that the course was challenging for cars of that era, the finishing straight being quite a steep uphill slope. Only one car – a Lynx – struggled to make the climb, with the driver having to get out and push!

In his book, *Ten Years of Motors and Motor Racing*, Charles Jarrott hints at a number of motorsport events taking place at Crystal Palace in 1899, and relays this account of the May event:

"The following month in May, the Motor Car Club, which then had as its secretary Mr F. W. Bailey, arranged a very exciting

Racing on the cycle track in 1901.

meeting. The entire grounds of the Crystal Palace were given over to the event, and a circular course mapped out. The cars and cycles were classified, and some very interesting racing took place. The event partook of a series of control tests and I think I succeeded in winning the class confined to motor cycles assisted by pedalling. The great event of the afternoon was the race for the Motor Car Club Championship ..."

The May event is described in some detail as a race between the tricycles of C. G. Wridgeway, S. F. Edge and Jarrott. Edge's machine never arrived so the race was between Jarrott and Wridgeway. Jarrott's account of the event describes the simple banked oval layout of the course: " ... again and again Wridgeway came out on the straight at each side of the track to endeavour to pass me, and again and again, grimly holding on to the position I had secured, I was able to retain my lead. The speed seemed terrible, and the enormous crowd watching the race gave vent to their excitement in terrific cheering."

In the end Jarrott won by little more than a wheel, later writing that it was one of the most exciting races he had ever taken part in.

Jarrott's time was the best of the day, and he was to taste success again as a five mile invitation motorcycle race was to be held on the oval cycle track. Alongside the invitation race was a match race between Edge and Wridgeway. These races were meant to start at around half-past five but didn't actually begin until after six. Four entrants took the start at the invitational: Charles Jarrott and C. G. Wrigeway on Asters, up against J. W. Stocks on a De Dion, and H. E. Zacharias on a Barriere tricycle. Jarrot won from Wridgeway, while the other two failed to finish.

A further event that year was a smaller affair in September, confined to the cycle track. It was made clear that some competitors were not welcome with their usual mounts, on account of " ... the terror which their speed prowess has engendered". As the usual

Close racing into Stadium Dip in the late 1930s. Note the grandstands and crowds along the Stadium Straight.

trio of Jarrott, Edge and Wridgeway entered it must be presumed that they acquired slower machines on which to compete. In the end only these three entered the race which became a straight fight between the De Dions of Jarrott and Edge. Wridgeway's Phebus Astor was off the pace and it quickly became obvious that he wasn't in the running.

Jarrott took the win in a popular manner, setting up the leader, Edge, on the run out of the final turn. Jarrott took the win by less than three inches (7.6cm). Edge got his own back in the one mile handicap when he and Jarrott were in a close contest for the entire race, Jarrott regaining the twenty feet lost at the start. The pair crossed the line in a dead heat. Edge won the run off by less than a wheel, after taking the inside line on the final bend,

These early meetings often evolved into a dice between the leading pioneers of British motorsport. Charles Jarrott's book *Ten Years of Motors and Motor Racing* covers most of these and is well worth a read.

During the first year of the Edwardian reign motorised sport continued in Joseph Paxton's 'second home' of Crystal Palace at Norwood Heights. On 8 April, 1901 the London suburbs around Norwood Heights rang to the distinct roar of motor competition.. A 1 mile speed trial was run by the English MC within the park, and the event was won by the venue's most succesful competitor at that point, Charles Jarrott, this time in an 8hp Panhard in 2m 16.6. A repeat event on 27 April was won by C. S. Rolls in a 24hp Mors, albeit on a much shorter course of just 350 yards (320 metres).

And that was it for a fair few years. The Palace lay quiet until the 1920s when that distinctive roar was once again heard.

During the early twenties the loose surface paths and tracks of country houses had been arranged to form a number of small

motorcycle tracks. These were club venues and would probably be the equivalent of the smaller club motorcycle tracks of today, or what Lydden Hill circuit is to cars. Events were run all over England on these smaller tracks, and notable venues included Drayton Manor, Esholt Park and Syston Park.

In 1926 a group of motorcycle enthusiasts gathered together by Fred Mockford and Cecil Smith formed London Motor Sports Ltd, with the aim of bringing back closed circuit racing to London. The group soon saw the potential of Crystal Palace park as a motor racing venue and, in 1927, approached the trustees of the park. After some persuasion permission was granted for a race meeting to be organised.

Early one Sunday morning a group of racers was invited to try out the proposed course made up of the park's pathways. They loved it and on May 21, 1927 the inaugural Crystal Palace road racing event occurred. Comprising a 10 race bill, all races were open to members of clubs in the South Eastern centre of the ACU (Auto Cycle Union). The course was a mix of hard packed but still loose surface sections linking tarred bends. The start/finish line was on the centre walk from where it ran roughly straight and slightly uphill to the Maze Hairpin, an ultra-tight left-hand corner popular with spectators. The track ran straight for a short distance and then turned through a greater than 90 degree right-hand corner known as Three Tree Bend.

Another tight right-hander – 'New Zealand' – followed after a short uphill straight. (It was named New Zealand because of the New Zealand Embassy replica which sat in the park near the track.) New Zealand opened into a long left-hand sweep that was ended by a super tight right-hand corner called the Statue Hairpin. Another left-hand sweep led uphill into Rockhills Hairpin, a right-hander which led onto a fast downhill section past the lake. Lastly, a right-hand sweep took the track behind the sports ground and back to the start/finish line.

Cars returned to racing at Crystal Palace in around 1928 when midget racers took to the oval cinder track used for speedway – it didn't go down very well with the speedway crowd, out to see their beloved Glaziers team perform.

Much of this 'path' course has been obliterated over the years though tantalising shreds remain. Rockhills Hairpin was renamed Pond Hairpin, and the fast downhill section that followed it

Crystal Palace 1937-1939.

became Fisherman's Rise; both of these have survived the park's tumultuous existence.

The next major development at the circuit heralded a halcyon period for the venue. In the mid-thirties rumours began in the motoring and sporting press of a 'Donington for London'. The general manager of the park's trustees, Sir Henry Buckland, had decided that a proper motor racing circuit could bring back the huge crowds that had visited in the past for both the path racing and also the speedway, which attracted crowds in excess of 70,000, more than a modern day Premier League football match!

A design proposal of a 2¼ mile (3.6km) circuit that skirted the edge of the park more or less, with a sinuous 'inner' loop around the maze, was first rumoured in 1935. The rumour turned out to be true; a 2 mile (3.21km) track had been designed by architect C. L. Clayton. Development of this track would determine the layout of the park right up until the present day.

And what a track it was. The starting grid was situated on a gentle right-hand kink; the starter's flag would drop and the mixed grid of ERAs, Maseratis and Rileys would leap forward and accelerate down the Stadium Straight, blasting over the stadium access subway. Spectators on the speedway bank got a great view of the field as it drifted its way into a fast right-hand sweep at the end of the straight known as Ramp Bend. The track then climbed up the ultra-tricky and fast Ramp Straight and Maxim Rise sections, to this day still deceptive, nearly catching me out as I researched this project when I encountered a dawdling Renault coming in the opposite direction. At the top of Maxim Rise the track passed under the spectator access bridge from the low level train station (Crystal Palace had two train stations; high and low level), then curved right at South Tower Corner onto the ultra long Terrace Straight. In the shadow of the grand Crystal Palace the terrace straight would often witness cars of the day exceeding 130mph (209kph). The straight swept gently left at the end and then into the especially long, spectacular and challenging right-hander that was North Tower Crescent, which led into perhaps one of the most beautiful parts of any race circuit I've ever visited.

After the sweep of North Tower the track meandered downhill through an alley of overhanging trees, the Glade, which make it difficult to believe that you are in South London. It must have been incredible to drive through this dark avenue at speed. It was fast but was ended by the tight right-hander at Fisherman's Bend, so called as the track skirts one of the park's lakes still popular with anglers. Out of Fisherman's Bend the track sweeps left along the lakeside and then turns tight-ish right at the confusingly named (given the name of the previous turn) Fisherman's Corner. The track runs uphill towards the Italianate

to New Zealand Hill. This right-hander was known as 'the link'.

Three days before construction of the circuit was due to start, a catastrophe struck South London. On November 30, 1936 Crystal Palace burnt to the ground, leaving little more than a gaunt-looking iron skeleton. Even so, work on the new circuit began on time and, within 5 months of the fire, the new circuit was ready. On 24 April, 1937 the first meeting took place and the opening race was won by a Pat G. Fairfield in his works ERA; he also established the lap record for the new circuit, averaging 54.59mph (87.85kph).

The circuit ran with great success, and many 'names' raced there, including Prince Bira who made Crystal Palace his own. Richard Seaman, who raced for the great works Mercedes Benz outfit, brought his W125 Silver Arrows to the Palace and drove a few demonstration laps. The circuit closed in 1939 at the outbreak of war with Raymond Mays in his ERA setting a final lap record of 60.97mph (98.11kph) a couple of months before the start of hostilities.

Most of this circuit remains today. Two sections are missing: the first, from halfway round Big Tree Bend all the way to the exit of Stadium Curve, was destroyed by the extensive work in the park in the 1970s; the other section to go was the middle 200 meters (218yds) of the Terrace Straight.

It took the park 8 years to recover from the war and for motor racing to return. Local residents were none too keen to see the return of racing at the Palace and kicked up a fuss, with the result that racing was restricted to just 5 days per year. The track, too, was changed as the inner loop was deemed too slow; a new link was added between Fisherman's Bend and the exit of Stadium Curve. New Link, as it was known, was a steep 1-in-8 drop which made the preceding Fisherman's Bend much faster. The start/finish line was resited halfway along the Stadium Straight, and safety was improved by new barriers.

The 'new' Crystal Palace opened on Whit Monday 1953 and attracted over 40,000 spectators. The fresh road racing course proved much faster, with Tony Rolt in his Connaught lapping at an average speed of 72.73mph (117kph). The circuit was from then on firmly on the motorsport map, holding regular Formula 2 meetings throughout its existence as well as many other car and bike events.

terraces that dominate the land between the Terrace Straight and the site of the Palace itself.

Following the path of the 1920s circuit right up to the left-handed Rockhills Hairpin – now known as Pond Hairpin – the track then swept right and turned left at Big Tree Bend down New Zealand Hill. The name of the hill is another hangover from the 1920s, though the track at this point does not follow the old course.

At the bottom of New Zealand hill the track turned left through stadium dip then down a short unnamed straight into a long right-hander at Stadium Curve. On the exit of this corner the field flashed past the timing box, over the grid, and began another lap.

There was also the option of a shorter circuit with a right-hand curve about halfway along the Terrace Straight linking the straight

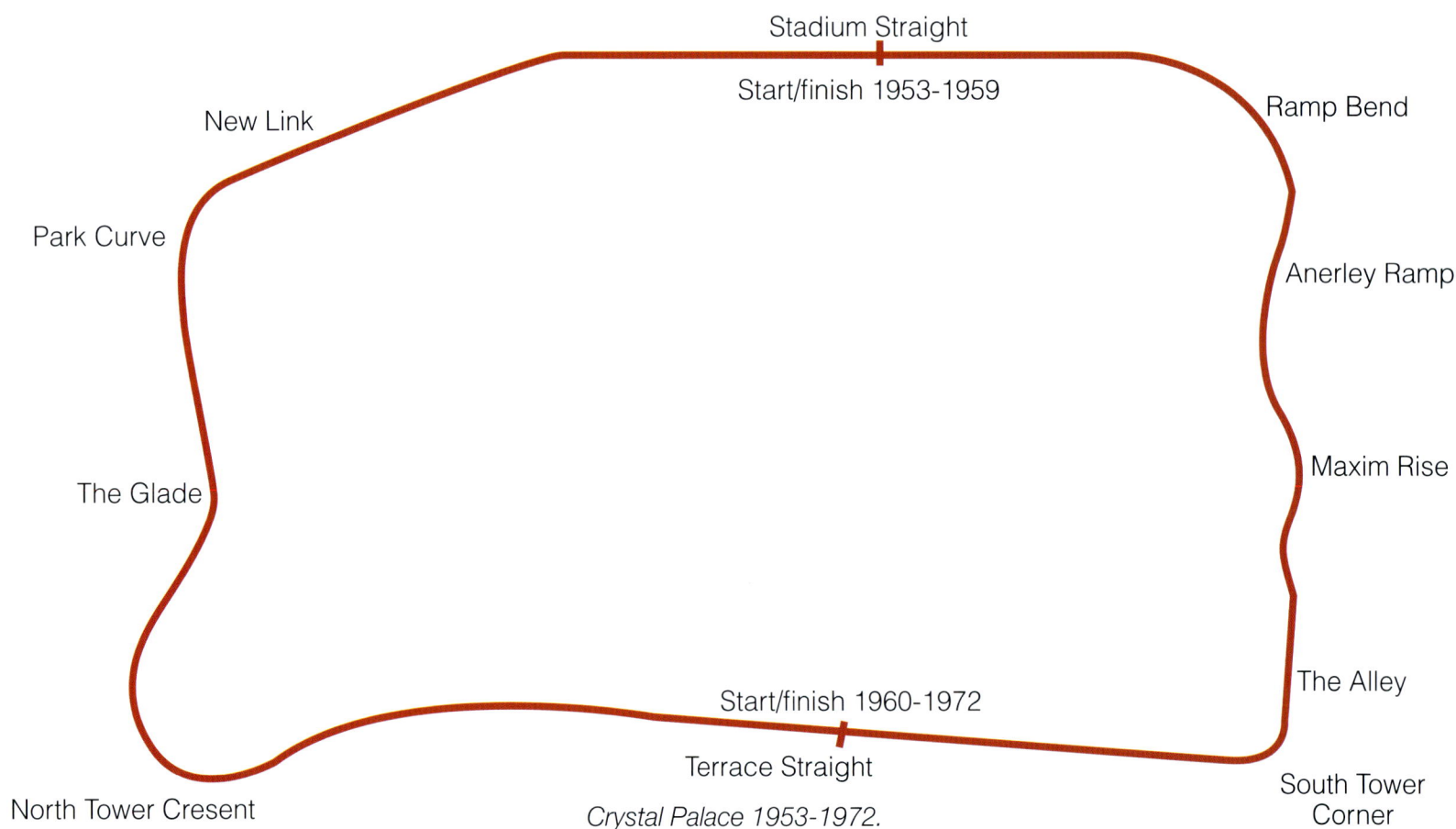

Stadium Straight

Start/finish 1953-1959

New Link

Ramp Bend

Park Curve

Anerley Ramp

Maxim Rise

The Glade

The Alley

Start/finish 1960-1972

North Tower Cresent

Terrace Straight

South Tower
Corner

Crystal Palace 1953-1972.

Further changes in the 1960s meant the start/finish line was repositioned on the Terrace Straight and can even be seen in that classic film caper *The Italian Job* complete with crashing Minis! These latter changes were to allow the construction of the new national sports centre.

In the early 1970s it was becoming clear that Crystal Palace was growing too fast and dangerous to run modern cars as average lap speeds were beginning to exceed 100mph (160kph), and run-off was non-existent. Suggested safety improvements would cost £250,000. Thing were not looking good for 'London's own circuit' ... At the start of 1972, after Mike Hailwood had set the final circuit lap record at a breakneck 103.39mph (166.35kph) in a Surtees-Ford, the Greater London Council announced that the circuit would close at the end of the season.

Crystal Palace seemed to be lost forever to motorsport, but in 1997 Sevenoaks and District Motor Club brought back the sport. On the May bank holiday it ran a speed hillclimb using parts of both pre- and post war circuits, and also created two new corners. The new speed course started near the top of Fisherman's Rise and followed the prewar inner loop up to where Big Tree Bend headed left before the outbreak of

war. Now there was a new corner, a tight right-hand hairpin – Duckhams Big Tree Bend – which connected the prewar inner circuit to the Terrace Straight in a mirror image of 'the link'. The cars then ran down the straight for a short distance to another new turn, Parfitts Chicane, a classic chicane which turned sharp right onto the outside of the Pond/Rockhills Hairpin, then sharp left back onto the Straight. The finish line was tucked away in the Glade.

The event ran annually for four years until Bromley Council began work on the park. The last ever motorsport event at Crystal Palace took place on Monday 29 May, 2000 – a bank holiday, as was the tradition for events at the Palace. As all who attended fully expected to return in 2001 the venue faded away with little more than a fizzle, with the council notifying the organising club just months before the 2001 event was due to take place. Sevenoaks and District Motor Club's magazine, the *Acorn*, ran a front page feature entitled 'Crystal Palace RIP'.

Council work carried out on the circuit consisted of halving the width of part of the old circuit, and adding a white surface; the affected areas are Parfitts Chicane, North Tower Crescent, the Glade, Fisherman's Bend and Fisherman's Rise.

CRYSTAL PALACE ROAD CIRCUIT

Brockbank

PROGRAMME
FOR THE
**Crystal Palace Cup
Meeting**
1st JULY, 1939
PRICE 1/-

Programme from 1 July, 1939 – Crystal Palace Cup Meeting, the penultimate meeting run on the 2 mile (3.21km) road racing course. The simple two-colour design depicts the front end of the racer, and one of the two towers that remained after the Palace burnt down. The content includes a witty look at some of the racing incidents and racers of the day. A small tribute to popular racing driver Richard Seaman, who had recently been killed during the Belgian Grand Prix, appears along with the running order and entry lists.

community, as a visit to any one of the pubs close to the circuit will confirm.

Residents who, for thirty years, have generally forgotten about the old track are being reminded of it by local enthusiasts and the local paper. In October 2003 the *News Shopper* ran a large story in its sports section entitled 'Big drive for return of motor racing festival.' The following week *Motorsport News* featured a story entitled 'Crystal Balls.' Both articles were about attempts by Sevenoaks Motor Club to restart speed hillclimbs at the circuit, though I suspect that its attempts will be unsuccessful, regretfully ...

A fair amount of the circuit remains today. The Stadium Straight is now used by Sport England as a car park, and the original circuit retaining wall is intact with a just-about-readable Dunlop advert. Ramp Bend right up to Maxim Rise has barely changed though the surface is breaking up in places and is in a poor state generally. South Tower Curve has been maintained as it forms part of the park's access to the national sports centre car park.

Rather than follow the line of the Terrace Straight the road swings away right and into a car park, and the straight is buried under a large pile of rubbish from recent work in the park. Before that it had been grassed over. Where the straight re-emerges near Big Tree Bend the surface has been damaged through neglect, and heavy plant parking on it has cut a number of gouges. As mentioned earlier recent action by Bromley Council has halved the width of a chunk of the track in the 'Concert Bowl' section; the original surface has been destroyed in this section also.

Visiting Crystal Palace is strange as the entire area has an overwhelming aura of dereliction and decay, from the vast empty train station to the decrepit Victoriana and overgrown Palace site. Situated in South East London the remnants of the circuit are now all within the confines of Crystal Palace park. Trains to Crystal Palace station are fairly frequent (which overlooks Maxim Rise); turn right out of the station, through the open turnstiles and you're on the spectator bridge over Maxim Rise. You wouldn't know that a motor race had ever taken place there, and even on the track there's little to see, apart from a burnt-out moped lying on the

... and now

There are currently plans to reinstate the sport at the venue but only time will tell if they come off. The plan is central to new initiative to bring more minority groups into the sport, as Crystal Palace is now surrounded by a thriving and multicultural

Blast off! Packed stands on the Terrace Straight watch the start of an early 1970s Formula 2 race.

spectator bank overlooking Maxim Rise: kind of fitting, in a way.

Crystal Palace was once a great place, and not only for motor racing; it also hosted the FA cup final, many exhibitions and events in the Palace itself and its grounds. Now it straddles the line between urban park and desolate wasteland. It's not only lost its reputation as a motor racing venue, but seems to have lost its soul, too. The small museum holds a few fragmented memories but little else. There's no mood, no ambience, no life; just a park with a melancholy air inhabited by Albino squirrels, distant memories, and Victorian ruins.

Ronnie Peterson sliding through North Tower Crescent during the 1971 Formula 2 meeting.

An early seventies F2 race gets under way – and the cars blast towards North Tower. (Courtesy Dave Marshall)

Anatomy of a drift. Formula 2 racers slither through North Tower during one of the last race meetings at Crystal Palace.

KEIMOLA

Keimola is a forgotten place, lost in a forest just outside of Helsinki, it is the very definition of dereliction. No longer with a purpose to serve, it once played host to world champions in their howling racers, charging down the long straights, desperate to better each other. Now it's simply wasteland, trees pushing their way up through its scarred and disfigured surface as nature reclaims its own.

As I'd not heard of this Finnish circuit I asked Paul Fearnley, editor of *Motorsport* magazine, if he had. He rummaged through a selection of excellent track maps but came up blank; then, an idea: "Interserie," he suggested, referring to the sports prototype racing series of the 1970s. That Keimola should be included in this book was not my idea but that of a young Dutch chap who had been helping me research the remains of the Nürburgring Sudschleife. I trawled the internet to find out more about this track not far from the centre of Helsinki and soon discovered a veritable goldmine of sources and information.

Construction of the track was started in 1965 by Curt Lincoln, Finland's top racer of the 1950s, and the man responsible for the circuit's planning. Keimola was Finland's first 'proper' permanent track, for a nation fast becoming obsessesed with motorsport.

The Keimolan Moottorstadion opened on 12 June, 1966; 3.3km (2.05 miles) in length with a number of constant radius corners, some slightly banked. The circuit was dominated, however, not by on-track action or its unique layout, but by the centrepiece of the venue, an eye-catching race control tower overlooking the huge main straight and pits complex. The track was built on an undulating piece of land, the highest point of which was 14 metres (45ft) above the lowest. This incline (on the straight after a slow corner) made the circuit particularly suited to more powerful cars, especially as the huge straight allowed for some very high speeds indeed. Looking at a track map the layout resembles a modern kart track, but don't let its simple layout deceive you: Keimola was a challenge!

During that opening meeting in June races were held for a variety of saloon cars; also Formula Vee and Formula 3. The Formula Vee race was run over 15 laps and was won by Sven-Olov Gunnarsson. The circuit quickly became a highly active place, and a wide variety of classes and race types took place over the years. Motorcycle and sidecar racing was common and, in 1968, endurance racing arrived. The Keimola 500 attracted a fairly mixed bag, Leo Kinnunen and Hans Laine winning in 4hrs 30m 35.9s, completing 152 laps. Their Porsche 911 beat off

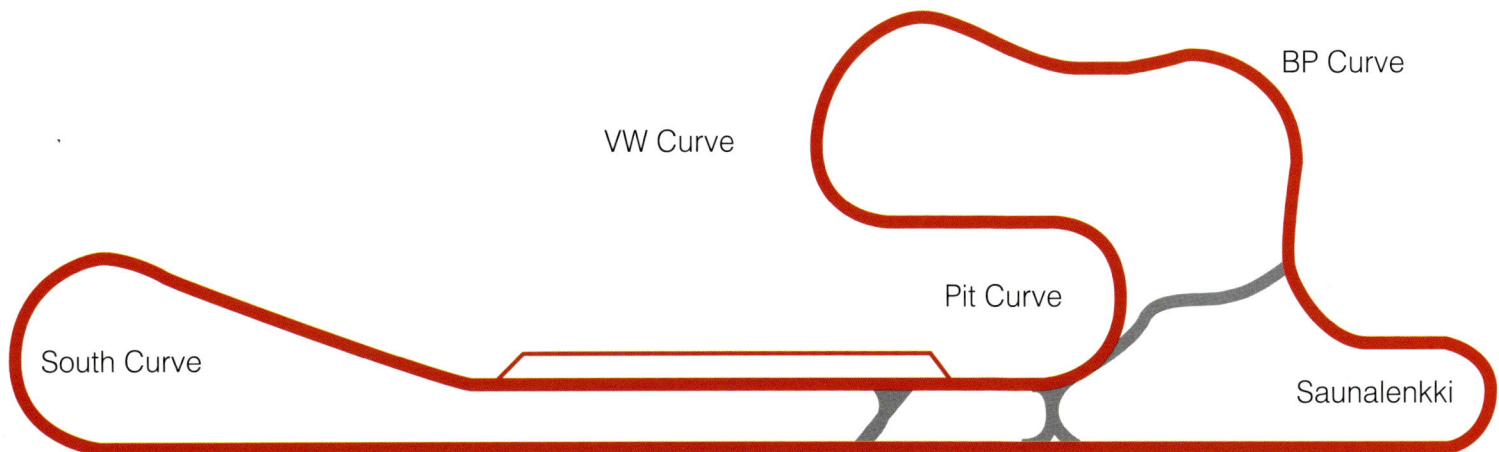

Keimola circuit had a constant layout for racing throughout its usage, differing only for rallycross events.

Interserie racers blast past the control tower in 1970, a Porsche 917 leading.

challengers ranging from Minis and NSUs to a similar 911, and most things in-between. Endurance racing became part of the track's fabric, and Keimola later hosted the big endurance racers of the Interserie.

On the track, hammering down the long main straight in your 'big banger' Porsche 917, the first challenge is the long banked, right-handed constant radius Southern Curve which leads back on itself to a short straight back toward the pits. A flat out left and kink whips you past the pit entry, unusual in that it isn't located by the grid. Roaring down the pit straight towards Varikkokaarre, or Pit Curve, another slightly banked constant radius corner, this time a left-hand semicircle. Heading along a short straight toward the paddock, the VW Curve, named after the stand there sponsored by VW, swings you right past the heli-pad. Before you even notice the 5ft (1.5m) high North State cigarette box advertising to your left you're heading right, through Curre's Curve No 1. The track then flows gently left again before the not-quite-flat-out Curre's Curve No 2 which throws you back to the right. (Curre's Curves are named after the track's founder Curt 'Curre' Lincoln.)

As soon as the car has left the right-hand Curre's section it's heading into BP Curve, a long downill left-hander. After BP Curve there's a tiny straight section before Saunalenkki, a tight, right-hand hairpin bend at the track's lowest point that leads back onto the long straight. The track heads uphill as soon as you exit the hairpin until you pass over the summit under the concrete arch festooned with Nestle sponsorship, and past the main stand to begin a new lap.

Curt Lincoln was also Jochen Rindt's father-in-law, and used this link to persuade Rindt to talk to some of his international racing rivals about Finland's new track. Lincoln was a determined fellow and, apparently, a persuasive one, too. In 1966, the circuit's first full year of existence, the Finnish Grand Prix was staged, and Jack Brabham, Jim Clark, Denny Hulme, Graham Hill and Rindt took part. The race was run, unusually, on a Wednesday evening, and was covered by *Autosport* magazine which takes up the story.

"One of the most exciting F2 races of the year was held at the new Keimola circuit outside Helsinki on Wednesday 24th August. At the end of both heats the Brabham Hondas of Jack Brabham and Denny Hulme were in front, with Jimmy Clark filling third place in the Ron Harris-Team Lotus Mk44 just ahead of Jochen Rindt in the Winklemann Brabham Cosworth. The race was divided into two heats of ten laps and 25 laps, with results based on the 35 lap aggregate. Brabham averaged 88.546mph over the 35 laps of the 2.049 mile long track."

With good light until well after 8pm it was quite feasible to have the race on a mid-week evening, although two factors affected attendance: many people were out of Helsinki on holiday, and the whole race was being televised, circuit owner and former Scandinavian champion, Curt Lincoln, having sold the TV rights. Although track construction had begun just four

The small Interserie field passes the pits – this was the view from the control tower.

Leo Kinnunen on his way to winning the 1971 Interserie race.

months previously, it was very near completion for the first ever full international race in Finland. It was well laid out with an abundance of pits, more paddock space than was necessary, a café for competitors, and a splendid control tower crowned by the three-pointed star of Mercedes Benz. One of the nicest touches of Curt Lincoln's organisation was to use members of the local judo club to marshal the course.

A few unusual names appeared on the F3 entry; Curt Lincoln took part but a big draw was rally star Timo Makinen in his first outing in a single seater. The event was a success and was repeated in 1967 with Jim Clark winning the F2 event from Rindt, Hill, Rees and Gardener. Jack Brabham retired due to problems with his fuel metering unit.

In 1969 the big sport racers arrived for the Nordic Challenge Cup. The field included Porsche 908s which set the scene for the really big cars of Interserie. The Porsche 917s and their rivals arrived in 1970. Keimola was round 4 of the 1970 series. Dutchman Gijs van Lennep won the 50 lap race in his 917K in just over an hour. Interserie returned in 1971 and '72; *Autosport* covered the 1971 race.

"Leo Kinnunen delighted the partisan crowd on Sunday when he took an AAW-sponsored Porsche 917 spyder to a convincing victory in both parts of the Interserie race, ahead of Peter Gethin in the Sid Taylor/Castrol McLaren M8E. Helmut Kelleners took the March 717 to third place and its best result after a good drive, while various troubles kept the rest of the small field out of contention. Kinnunen's win now puts him in a firm lead of the championship whilst Gethin moves up to second place".

As was expected, the fifth round of the Interserie Championship suffered the worst entry to date because, despite this race being obligatory in the points for the Championship, few thought it worth the long journey. The Keimola circuit is situated a few miles from Helsinki and, apart from one good straight of around 1km (1093yds), the rest of the circuit is a series of geometric curves which do not really suit G7 racing.

Kinnunen also won the last Interserie race at the circuit in 1972 in damp conditions driving the monstrous Porsche 917/10.

Rallying legend Pentti Airikkala took part in a number of races at Keimola, and remembers how he managed to win his first ever race there: "I was entered in the races at Keimola in a car for which I had no tyres. I had seen these fantastic American racing tyres advertised and decided to buy some. Because of the time it would take to get them to Finland I could only collect them from the airport the day before the race. When I got there I was horrified because they had sent me what I thought were some old, worn out tyres with no treads left but, because I had nothing else, I had to use them. Of course, I won the race easily and thought it was because I was a great driver when, in reality, it was the tyres. I had never seen slick tyres before – neither had anyone else in Finland at the time. I know better now!"

In the seventies a kart track was built behind the paddock and next to the Pit Curve. The new track witnessed the beginning of a future world champion's career: Mika Hakkinen went on to win the Formula One World Championship for McLaren in 1998 and 1999. Former Ferrari F1 driver Mika Salo was also active at the track and beat Hakkinen there on at least one occasion. Their rivalry was still apparent in Formula One many years later, the two Mikas still allegedly failing to see eye-to-eye!

During the 1970s the circuit's owners explored many avenues for its use in order to generate a good profit, which it was struggling to do. Drag racing, rallycross and even rock concerts were tried out, and a scaled-down 'Kiddie Keimola' (Pikku Keimola) was built near the pit entry, complete with ⅓ scale control tower. It wasn't enough; the track no longer had a major international meeting, no longer had a major spectator draw, no longer made a profit. Its time had run out.

Over the road from the memorial is an abandoned quarry, ruined structures and overgrown area reflecting the fate of the legendary race circuit that runs past its mutilated rock face. A long, haunting tone echoes around the surrounding forest – the siren of a neighbouring quarry bestows an uneasy atmosphere on the area.

Arrival of the track in Kohoutovice is sudden. After rising up out of the Farina section the wooded slopes alongside the road give way to the grim tower blocks of this 'satellite town'. Trolley busses rattle into a terminus, and the old course of the track is plain to see. The track sweeps off to the right on a long banked corner, now blocked to traffic and used as a car park. An old Skoda faces the wrong way down the track – gently rusting away to nothing. It's possible to make out the original white line markings along the side of the track continuing across what is now a busy road and up into the town.

Here, the circuits separate again, the post 1975 version heading off downhill after flinging the cars left and right, the blocks of flats rising up by the trackside protected by barriers. At the bottom of the hill a right-hand hairpin takes the racers to the pit straight.

The Masarykring has a forsaken ambience, its reason for existing consigned to history. The memory of screaming racers has faded, leaving just echoes of bygone events. A new 'safe' Masarykring is tucked away in a corner of the old circuit. As with most modern venues it's made up of short straights and slow corners bounded by vast gravel traps. It's a tame substitute, but the original circuit was a little too wild ...

An interesting aside is that, just a few hundred kilometres away in the Czech Republic's capital of Prague, Rudolf Carraciola's 1938 Mercedes Benz W125 Grand Prix car sits in the city's technical museum in unrestored condition. The famous Silver has faded and yellowed, giving the car a golden appearance, the remains of the three-pointed star all but completely faded away. Dents cover the bodywork of this iconic machine, giving it an abandoned and forgotten air. Much like the circuit it once raced on, the 'proper' Masarykring.

Whilst the new Masarykring is nowhere near as challenging or scenic as the old circuit which runs past its gates, echoes of times gone by still remain.

Hans
BALTISBERGER

MOTOCYKLOVÝ ZÁVODNÍK
NĚMECKÉ SPOLKOVÉ REPUBLIKY

* 16.9.1922
+ 26.8.1956

ALEŠ BILÍČEK

† 13. 4. 2003

JEN TI NEJRYCHLEJŠÍ UMÍRAJÍ PRVNÍ

AVUS

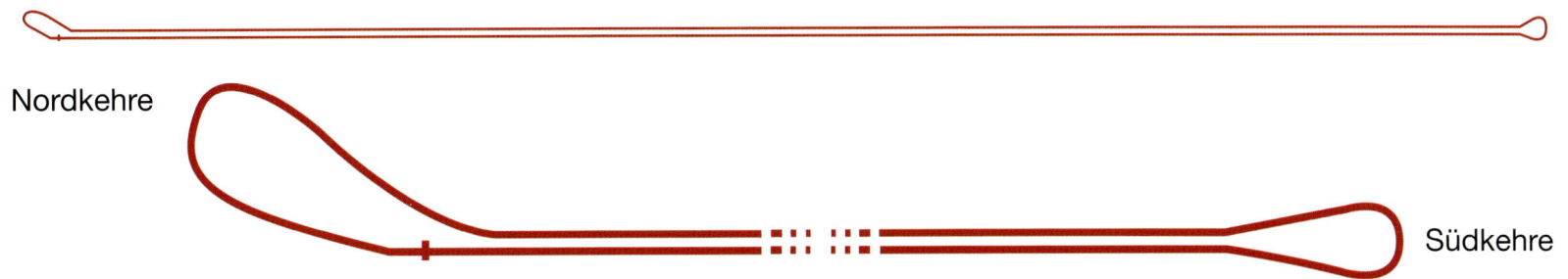

Nordkehre

Südkehre

The AVUS 1921-1939.

At Goodwood House near Chichester in mid-summer every year, when England is at its most glorious, the resident Lord March gives over the grounds for a celebration of motor racing history. At each of his Lordship's annual garden parties, an event known as the Festival of Speed, there is a fantastic sculpture, a new one every year, dedicated to a great period of the sport's history.

In the late 1990s the sculpture harked back to a darker period, shortly before the land around Goodwood House was requisitioned by the RAF, and long before Goodwood became connected with motorsport. The giant edifice was a stunning silver streamlined car rounding an impossibly banked corner, evoking a race run some sixty years earlier to exalt Germany's Nazi government. Barely a year after this politically charged motor race, the rattle of machine guns filled the air over Goodwood, as Hurricane and Spitfire fighter planes flew into combat from RAF Westhampnett, an airfield which went on to become another famous race circuit.

A leading tourist guide describes Berlin as being as exciting as Clacton-on-Sea; no surprise, then, that a quick glance at a map of Berlin's race circuit shows nothing to recommend it. Essentially two long straights joined by simple corners at each end, it's not the most thrilling circuit layout by any means, but potentially one of the fastest, though as modern Formula One shows us, speed alone does not necessarily equal excitement. However, photos of stunning Auto Union and Mercedes streamliners blasting around a perilously high 'Wall of Death' banking, watched by black uniformed men, tell a different story.

The Automobil Verkehrs und Übungs Strasse, or AVUS, was conceived around the same time as the Nürburgring, and for very similar reasons. In 1907 the Kaiser watched an Italian win a Gordon Bennett race held in the Taunus mountains. As a result he was moved to found the Kaiser Automobile club (which later became Automobile Club von Deutschland – AvD). His support for the new sport continued, and he felt a motor vehicle test track was required in the capital city of Berlin. The track was to be built between the Charlottenburg area of Berlin and Nickolasee just outside the city.

A 19.6km (12.17 mile) track was constructed: two huge straights linked by lightly banked return loops at each end formed the circuit. The Northern Curve was known as Nordkehre and the Southern as Südkehre. It was not a complex affair – the two straights were parallel, separated by a strip of grass just a couple of metres wide.

The precise date of the first race seems to have been lost over the years; not surprising, considering the tumultuous period that began in Berlin in 1945. It's been said that the AVUS is the world's first motorway, operating as a toll road before the First World War, during which all motorsport activity ceased.

The track was not used for racing between the end of the First World War and 1921, when work instigated by one Hugo Steinnes to bring back racing was completed. The first race after the war was won by Fritz von Opel, fittingly enough in an Opel. The entire grid was made up of German cars. AVUS was to become all about German supremacy.

Five years later the track played host to the inaugural German Grand Prix, and 220,000 people turned up to see the race. With cars achieving speeds of 200mph (321.86kph) the spectacle must have been incredible, especially as the race was run in pouring rain. Rudi Carraciola won the race for Mercedes, which forever earnt him the reputation of regenmeister (rain master).

The depression brought about a lull, with little in the way of motorsport for a few years, with the exception of a few record attempts in 1928. During this period the National Socialist party grew apace, its leader, Adolf Hitler, in the ascendancy. At some point Hitler was introduced to racing driver Hans Stuck who, along with others, impressed upon the fast rising politician the importance of motor racing as a propaganda tool.

Racing returned in 1932, and once again huge crowds turned out on a regular basis to watch the increasingly fast and streamlined cars. Germany was at the beginning of a new era of motorsport, a fact drummed home at the 1933 Berlin Motor Show held just a few miles away, when Hitler – now Chancellor – gave a speech stressing how important motorsport was to the German nation.

129

Bernd Rosemeyer holds all but one member of the crowd's attention as he rounds the banking at 125mph (201kph) in his streamlined Auto Union during the 1937 Avusrennen. (Courtesy Erhard Benad)

So it was that construction work began on Nordkehre and racing was halted throughout 1936 so the work could continue. The result was a 92.6 degree radius bend, banked at an alarming 43.6 degrees. The banking rose to 12.42 metres (40.74ft) and was surfaced with brick paving – making it treacherous in the wet. Many drivers struggled to get anywhere near the top, and eventually a white line was added, above which drivers were not allowed to go.

The track reopened on 30 May, 1937. Now complete with Hitler's 'wall of death', circuit length was 19.3km (11.99 miles). It was the fastest track in the world – and remained so for three more decades.

That late May meeting, the 1937 Avusrennen race meeting that was also a major Nazi propaganda event, was to be a big one. Entries included 2 W25K-M125 Streamliner Mercedes Benz to be driven by Carraciola and Lang; von Brauchtisch in a Mercedes W25K-DAB 5.6L Streamliner; Rosemeyer in an Auto Union C type, and a brace of private Maseratis. The Scuderia Ferrari Alfa Romeos withdrew before the meeting. Well over a quarter of a million people turned up to spectate, and it was clear who the controlling body was from the large number of swastika flags fluttering in the breeze.

The warm, early summer's day dawned perfectly. Josef Goebbels, Minister for Propaganda, took his seat in the stand to watch the voiturette race and the three heat Avusrennen. The entry, too, seemed to be all about German supremacy: "Without exaggeration, there was gathered at the Berlin track easily the fastest group of racing cars in the world. Four Auto Unions,

Adolf Hitler's influence on motorsport can still be seen in the sport today in the fact that Silver Arrows still appear at the front of the Grand Prix grid ... but that's a book in itself. Legend has it that in 1935 he watched Mercedes Benz win the Avusrennen at an average speed of 238.5kph (148.2mph). It's said that during this meeting Hitler himself suggested that the two turns be fully banked to increase average speeds. Germany, he demanded, should have the world's fastest race circuit ...

Hermann Lang – winner of the 1937 Avusrennen – passes the Mercedes building in his W25K-M125 Mercedes Benz streamliner. Note the swastika behind Lang's head. He was later received on the podium by Josef Goebbels. (Courtesy Erhard Benad)

two of them ultra-streamlined models, and five Mercedes Benz, three of them fully streamlined with enclosed wheels and two with the new 12 cylinder engine." enthused the *Autocar*. The Avusrennen was without doubt a showcase for German engineering excellence. All of the top European teams, such as Scuderia Ferrari, had pulled out or failed to enter in the face of German might at the last major race in Tripoli a few weeks before. Despite this there were still nine highly competitive works cars on the entry list, and a large cash prize awaited the winner. German glory was assured, however, as the fastest works drivers were Germans and they had the best equipment. English Mercedes pilot Dick Seaman had to cope with the previous year's unstreamlined model.

The race meeting was run with 2 heats and a final, providing the crowd with maximum entertainment. The races were hard-fought slipstreaming affairs with cars passing and re-passing each other up to five times a lap. During the first of these heats

Bernd Rosemeyer clinched the record for the AVUS as the world's fastest race circuit, lapping at 276.39kph (171.78mph) in his Auto Union which was running poorly, on 13 cylinders only, which begs the question: could he have gone quicker in a healthy car? The winner of the event was Hermann Lang in his Mercedes, after surviving a serious moment during practice. He described it after the event:

"During practice we tried the streamliners with covers over the wheels. Those at the front were fairly wide to allow the wheels to turn in the bends at either end of the circuit, and on one run I was doing about 245mph (394.27kph) when the front of the car began to lift and all I could see was the sky! I immediately thought, 'I must not move the steering, for if the front wheels return to the road in a different position there is bound to be an accident'. Luckily there was no crosswind and I backed off the throttle very carefully, but it was a long time before the front wheels touched the ground again.

132

Englishman Dick Seaman chases Lang around the banking during the 1937 Avusrennen. Seaman was in the older and unstreamlined W125 Mercedes racer. (Courtesy Erhard Benad)

"I must admit this incident gave me quite a fright and I stopped at the pits, white-faced and said 'For heaven's sake take those covers off!' The air was getting trapped inside the wheelarches and it was like having two balloons under there. The covers were removed and I had no more problems. Needless to say the wheels stayed uncovered for the race."

The following year the Südkehre was moved further north, reducing the track length. During the latter years of the 1930s the road was converted from toll to public usage, and in 1940 was connected to the autobahn network.

In his 1939 book, *Motor Racing,* Earl Howe gives a description of Berlin's own circuit.

"This track consists of two straights, both of them rather narrow – I should think not more than 25 to 30ft broad – about 6 miles long, with a very small radius curve at the Potsdam end, fairly steeply banked, and large radius curve at the Berlin end, which has now been so steeply banked that it almost approaches the idea of that popular entertainment 'The wall of death'. The two legs of the circuit are separated by a grass strip in the middle; the grass strip is only 10 to 15 yards wide, and there is a danger that if a car should get into difficulties owing to a tyre burst, or hitting another car on one leg of the circuit, it may charge across and hit cars coming in the opposite direction. I do not think this has ever happened, but it did very nearly happen on one

The 1937 Avusrennen was supported by a voiturette race for 1.5 litre cars; here, one gets close to the photographer. (Courtesy Erhard Benad)

133

Nordkehre

Südkehre

The AVUS 1951-1988.

Nordkehre

Südkehre

The AVUS 1988-1993 (Bremskehre added in 1992).

Nordkehre

Bremskehre

Südkehre

The AVUS 1994-1999.

The circuit played host to DTM races, which saw the great battles of Auto Union, Mercedes, and Alfa Romeo rekindled.

occasion a few years ago. The road goes through a forest and there are gaps in the trees , and if there is a side wind blowing it is well to remember this, because you may emerge from an area of calm air into strong wind, and this may make things difficult for the owner of a very fast car.

"The spectators are able to come quite close up to the track, and if a car did by any chance get into difficulties, a most serious accident, perhaps involving hundreds of spectators, could easily take place.

"From the driver's point of view under bad conditions of weather the track can get very slippery. Owing to the turns taking place at the end of long straights, it is essential for the driver to know the braking points and for his brakes to be beyond suspicion. The surface of the turn at the Berlin end was surfaced with brick and, I believe, still is, and a driver ought to remember that, as Indianapolis has shown us, slight oil droppings on a brick surface produce one of the worst skid surfaces in the world."

The war put a stop to racing for obvious reasons. When US troops arrived they found the circuit badly damaged, with a collapsed bridge blocking part of it. During a visit by President Truman, the circuit which once served to promote German superiority was used as a parade ground for the victorious American soldiers.

It wasn't until 1951 that the AVUS returned to the racing scene, after a group, led by Kurt Linder, got things going again. Mercedes returned in force three years later in 1954, fielding the über team of Juan Manuel Fangio, Karl Kling and Hans Hermann. However, at the 1955 Le Mans 24 hours race a works Mercedes flew off the track and killed a large number of spectators as well as driver Pierre Levegh. This tragedy caused the company to abandon all racing activity; works cars from Mercedes Benz did not return for years.

For a few years the circuit was used only for national racing, but Grand Prix racing was to make a return in 1959 when Lotus, Ferrari, Cooper and BRM were all represented. The meeting was a tragic one as local French favourite Jean Behra went over the top of the banking in his Porsche and was killed instantly. Hitler's wall of death had lived up to its nickname ...

At that race meeting Stirling Moss gave an interview, and one of the questions he was asked was: "Do you consider this (the

AVUS) a safe circuit? Moss replied: "No, I don't. It's very unsafe – it's very unsatisfactory – it's uninteresting – it proves nothing, and I think it's a great shame when in Germany they have one of the worst tracks in the world, and possibly one of the best tracks in the world (the Nürburgring), but they pick the worst and run it (the Grand Prix) there". He continued "I suppose it's political and I think that I'm in with all the other drivers who agree with me that we think this is a very bad, unsatisfactory and untesting course as far as the drivers are concerned and not worthy of a World Championship race." The interview was given before the death of Jean Behra. The AVUS never hosted the German Grand Prix again as in 1960 it moved to the Nürburgring Südschleife. Moss was roundly slated in the German press for criticising the circuit and retiring on the first lap of the race.

In 1967 the Nordkehre banking was demolished to allow a new motorway junction to be built – the new corner followed the same course as the old but was flat except for a slight camber. The circuit was closed between 1967 and reopened in 1971, now measuring 8.1km (5.033 miles). This configuration was used for 20 years and the track ran races for everything ranging from F3 to DTM, and even the big sportscars of Interserie.

The final curtailment of the circuit occurred in 1989 when another Südkehre was built much closer to the pits. The circuit now measured just 2.64km (1.64 miles). The vastly popular German touring car championship (DTM) visited on an annual basis until in 1995 a number of huge shunts culminated in a multiple car pile-up. The DTM teams – including some of the great works teams, Alfa Romeo, Mercedes and Auto Union (Audi) squads outfits, which were active on the circuit in the 1930s – left in disgust never to return.

Autosport reported the race, or, more precisely, the big crash:

"Pile-up halts Avus race; future in doubt?

The fourth round of the German Touring Car Championship was abandoned after a multiple pile-up left eight cars destroyed and called into question the safety of the AVUS autobahn circuit in Berlin. The crash – which also badly damaged another eight cars – occurred at the start of the second race when Alfa star Nicola Larini tried to squeeze his car between Keke Rosberg's Opel Calibra and Christian Danner's Alfa."

The article explained that many drivers had criticised Larini for trying an overtaking move that wasn't really on. But Larini felt the circuit was to blame. "It is too narrow; it is impossible to drive here in these circumstances. It should really be closed." Opel driver Manuel Reuter backed him up, claiming that if a car hit a barrier, it bounced back into the path of other cars, and soon the whole field was involved. Larini's comments were reminiscent of those made by Stirling Moss all those years before. This was the second big accident in a short period; just a few months earlier a car driven by John Winter destroyed some of the barriers and burst into flames. The track was modified following that shunt.

The DTM never returned, but its place was filled by Super Touring cars. However, the very nature of the circuit resulted in another multiple car smash – this time Audi driver Frank Biela hit the side of Kieth Odor's Nissan Primera, and the driver of the Japanese car was killed.

... and now

The AVUS was soon closed: the final meeting was an historic affair which celebrated the past, but for the future the main grandstand and the podium were preserved and covered by protection orders. The old Mercedes building remains intact, now in operation as a motel frequented mainly by truck drivers. The hotel has not forgotten its past, however, as the breakfast tables are made up of maps and images of the circuit in its heyday, whilst pictures of DTM Alfa Romeo adorn the walls.

The AVUS had a tumultuous existence. The banking long gone, the circuit still plays host to Audi (Auto Union) and Mercedes cars, but which now have more than one seat. A solitary grandstand watches over a busy stretch of autobahn, whilst the flagpole behind a winner's podium waits in vain for a winner's flag.

In the entrance to the building a large-scale recreation of a 1953 poster is painted on the wall. Looking out the window next to it you see the slowly rusting Armco barrier of the still intact Nordkehre. The course of the last evolution of the track is easy to follow – rusting triple layer Armco lines the roadside on both sides of the track. Behind the barrier lies the concrete retaining wall topped by a mesh fence of the type found at most modern circuits. The timing loop is still buried under the starting grid but there's no timing gear in the empty stand opposite.

The road runs down to the last evolution of the Südkehre; the track swings off the main carriageway to the right then turns sharply left back across the motorway to join the northbound carriageway. There's little past this point that distinguishes the AVUS as anything other than a busy dual carriageway. The road still follows the course of the track, but as you reach Nickolasse there is no sign of the first Südkehre.

Heading back up the northbound carriageway the Armco restarts and you can follow the way past the podium (now home to a large ant population!) and onto the approach to the Bremskehre chicane – now blocked by a rather makeshift Armco barrier. Bremskehre was added late in the life of AVUS in order to slow the Nordkehre. However, the corner is a snapshot of the circuit's final years. The old sawtooth kerbing, originally painted red and white, has flaked and faded, but it's still possible to see where cars clipped the apex as scuffs and tyre marks remain. The telltale sign of locked wheels is still there in the braking zone, amazingly – the old skid marks not quite washed away.

Behind the sawtooth curbing there remains a small and overgrown gravel trap, but the most evocative parts of the Nordkehre are the dents and scars on the Armco where errant cars were brought to an abrupt halt.

The AVUS today is one of the major routes into a nation's capital, a fast circuit where once drivers battled for the lead instead of battling against the morning traffic. The AVUS probably won't be forgotten – but it may well be ignored. Most people we spoke to considered the AVUS to be just a road; a famous road, to be sure, but still just a road. And I suppose that is all it is now, a road, with the paddock a lorry park: the AVUS may have lost its glory – but it hasn't lost its pride ...

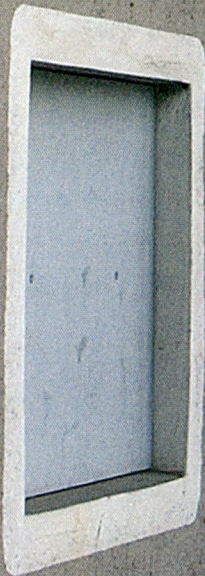

ZIMMER ab 24. mit Fri

MOTEL A

Agip

50 €
stück

VUS

RCEDES-BENZ
...innt auch den »Großen Preis von Berlin...
...nraum (50000...) ...der schnellsten Rennstrecke der Welt...

1. Karl Kling
2. Juan Manuel Fangio
3. Hans Herrmann

Das neue Verwaltungs-Gebäude

4./5. Mai 1991
ADAC-Avus-Rennen
Deutsche Tourenwagen-Meisterschaft • Formel 3
Opel Lotus Challenge • Formel Ford 1600
Shell. Ein Motor des Fortschritt...

ADAC-AVUS-Rennen
BERLIN
10.5.1987
INTER...
FIA-Coupe...
SUPER SPORTS C...
SPRINT-CHAMPION...
SACHS
BLAUPUNKT Cup
BLAUPUNKT

INTERNATIONALES ADAC
AVUS RENNEN
3./4. September '94, Berlin
Deutsche Tourenwagen Meisterschaft
Deutsche Formel 3 Meisterschaft
Ferrari 348 Challenge • Käfer Cup
elf MINOL
EIN STARKES TEAM

En...
GRO...

INTERNATIONALE
AvD · AVUS · RENN...

LINAS
MONTLHÉRY

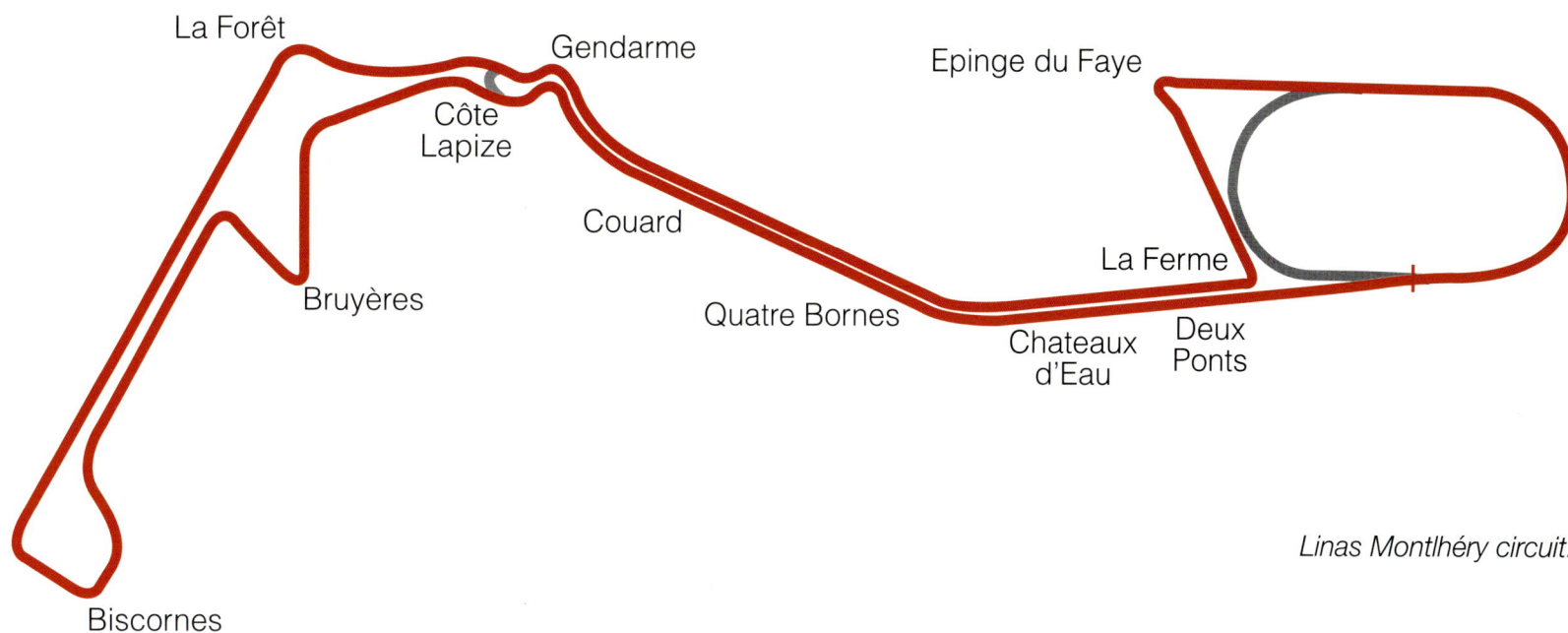

La Forêt
Gendarme
Côte Lapize
Epinge du Faye
Couard
La Ferme
Bruyères
Quatre Bornes
Deux Ponts
Chateaux d'Eau
Biscornes

Linas Montlhéry circuit.

The meeting was far, far behind schedule, but nobody complained as this would be the last chance that anyone would ever get to race on this combination circuit near Paris. Earlier in the day the 1000km de Paris was recreated, and the lucky few who gathered to watch saw a Lola T70 running high on the Piste De Vitesse banking to victory.

Linas Montlhéry hosted its final automobile race in June 2004. After eighty years of use, its owner, UTAC, took the decision to close it for competition use. But those eighty years were glorious ones!

In 1923 Alexandre Lamblin – an industrialist in the business of producing radiators for aeroplanes and automobiles – decided it was high time that France had a racing circuit which could compete with Brooklands, Indianapolis and Monza. Brooklands had been open for 12 years, the 'Brickyard' for 4, and Monza had just opened. Lamblin just had to act. He purchased a 12,000 acre slice of land on the Saint-Eutrope plateau a few miles south of Paris, and just outside the small town of Linas near Montlhéry.

With the land purchased two studies were commissioned to explore the possibility of a circuit, and, as usual in such matters, the least expensive option was chosen. This study envisaged a 2.5km (1.5 mile) track with potential for a longer road course outside the main track. Raymond Jamin was the man hired to design the course. On completion the banked oval course measured 2.548km (1.583 miles) around the centre line. The twin bankings were designed so that a car weighing a metric ton could run in the high groove at around 220kph (136.7mph).

In just six months the circuit was officially open. During the first two months of its life over one hundred records were established or beaten, with many of the cars and drivers coming from England. The English chose to compete here because of running restrictions at Brooklands, such as no night-time runs and silencer requirements. Gwenda Stewart was an early lap record holder, averaging 234.7kph (145.8mph) around the oval course in her Derby-Miller.

John Cobb described the course in the 1939 book *Motor Racing*; here, he compares it to the outer course at Brooklands.

"The fact there is no definite edge to Brooklands is always interesting, for if a fast car is travelling within two feet of the upper edge of the banking, it appears to its driver that the outer tyres are running actually on the edge, a somewhat intimidating experience. Montlhéry is much the same. The track, being newer and not used so continuously as Brooklands, has a better surface. The banking, being of later design, is higher. Nevertheless, the surface of the track tends to break up at times, and in any case possesses bumps, which though fewer are rather more shattering than those at Brooklands, and definitely have to be avoided during a long run for records. The banking, too, is more disquieting than that of Brooklands, because a considerable portion of the so-called retaining wall has been blown down, and when, therefore, the car travels close to the top of the banking, all the driver can see to his right side is the tops of a number of trees. Montlhéry's banking, I may say, is built up on concrete columns, and there's a sheer drop from its top to the ground.

"By some peculiarity of design, the track tends to cause a car to swerve badly inward just where the banking meets the straight, while the surface, though excellent in dry weather, is extremely slippery during or after rain."

For the 1925 season the planned road course was built, bringing total circuit length to 12.5km (7.76 miles). It was 10 metres (10.9yds) wide with a gradient of 1-in-8 at its most hilly. Surfaced with tar it came to rank amongst the world's greatest laps. The road course looks nothing special on a map, but it was seriously challenging. A high speed run-off – the Piste de Vitesse – brought cars screaming past the pits, then, rather than swinging back onto the banking to the right, the track ascended a slight hill and headed over the twin bridges at Les Deux Ponts. A very long fast straight ran up to a very fast right-hand kink at Les Quatre Bornes. High speed was the order of the day as the cars roared up another kilometre long straight, but a steep dip and steeper rise preceded the turn-in point for a fast right-hand sweep, the apex situated on a blind crest. The super quick sweep was followed by another steep drop with the tight left-handed Lacets de Couard at its base. The exit of Couard led into a right-hander which switched back to the left at the 3km (1.864 mile) post. As the car exited the left-hander here, the road simply dropped, the steep downhill gradient would leave any racer's stomach behind; it's daunting just to walk it.

At the bottom of the drop the road flicked to the left and onto another short straight. Epingle des Bruyères followed the straight and was a tight right corner – a hairpin, in effect. A short squirt on the power brought a tight left-hander before the long blast down to the left-right-right-right sequence of ever-tightening turns which made up the Garage des Biscornes loop. The final 90 degree right-hander led onto the 1.5km (1640yd) straight up to the tree-lined Virage de la Forêt. (The old entrance to the circuit is at the start of this straight.) Virage de la Forêt swung right and brought the course back uphill to shadow the earlier part of the lap. At the top of the hill a few sweeps led over the crest of the hill and down into the tight left-right section of Virage du Gendarme. From here the next two kilometres (1.2 miles) ran alongside the opposite leg of the circuit, back through Quatre Bornes and onto Deux Ponts where the course turned sharply left at the 10km (6.21 mile) post through Virage de la Ferme. The back of the Western Banking loomed to the right of the track as the cars headed up a straight and into the hairpin at Epingle Du Faye. From there the track ran straight and rejoined the Piste De Vitesse round the Eastern Banking, and onto a new lap.

The new section allied to the banking played host to the Automobile Club de France Grand Prix in 1925. This race was tinged with tragedy when Antonio Ascari became one of the road course's first victims; he was killed on the fast run towards Virage de la Ferme in his Alfa Romeo P2.

The ACF GP returned in the years between 1931 and 1937, with the exception of 1932. The circuit was in decline, however, and increasing operating costs and the condition of the track surface forced the administrators of the circuit to sell the entire 750 hectare site to the French government, which let the military take over. The track, like many others, was abandoned during the war and fell into decay.

The Grands Prix that ran during the thirties were marathon affairs. The 1931 race was run for two seaters, with only the driver in the car. Reserve drivers were also on hand as the race lasted 10 hours, with a start time of 8am! Louis Chiron and Achille Varzi, usually rivals, teamed up to contest the race. The pair beat off teams consisting of 'names' such as Nuvolari, Carracciola, Howe, Campari, and Biondetti.

Improvements to the circuit – and a 100,000 franc purse put up by the ACF – saw the big race return in 1933, this time to be run over 40 laps of the full circuit. In the following prewar years the race became a fixture at the circuit. The 1934 race bore witness to the early stages of the Auto Union/Mercedes Benz battle that continued for the next five years. The race was a classic and the *Autocar* reported on it with some verve.

"Of all the Grand Prix races, and their number is legion, there is none in the world to compare with the one, the only, original Grand Prix of the Automobile Club of France. Nor given a thousand years, could we create quite the atmosphere, the enchantment of that race.

"Consider the matter. From the earliest dawn hundreds upon hundreds of cars made their way cheerily to Montlhéry track, perched on a hilltop just off the road to Orleans, shimmering last Sunday in the sunshine. That famous little café, the Potiniere, speedily became crowded with all the nations gathered round tables sipping coffee or other drinks, discussing the coming fight eagerly with waiters only too anxious to voice opinions, or with Madame Berthot, whose knowledge of racing is both extensive and peculiar. She, by the way, held stoutly to the opinion that Alfa Romeo would win.

"This opinion seemed unlikely to be correct as the full force of German technology was being brought to bear on this corner of France: the Silver Arrows were in town. The Nazi funded racers of Mercedes Benz and Auto Union were the latest and most advanced competition cars ever built. The Scuderia Ferrari Alfa Romeos surely stood no chance …

"The setting was superb as the racing cars of France, Germany and Italy, thirteen in all, gathered for one of the greatest battles in history, and voluble teeming thousands settled in their seats. Montlhéry, it seemed, had grown more, many more trees, until one noticed those trees walked 'Dunsinane fashion'

The start of the 1934 French Grand Prix. Alfa Romeo Tipo B P3 leads Mercedes Benz W25. The race saw a real clash of the titans with Alfa Romeo, Bugatti, Auto Union and Mercedes Benz in a fight for supremacy in France.

as more and more people used whole saplings for shade. One individual, faun-like in appearance and tanned a rich shade of brown, had apparently completely discarded all his clothes in the scorching heat; a fire extinguisher "made itself go off" on the grandstand, generating tremendous hilarity, whilst, over it all, the ACF flag proudly flew upside down on the great pole above the press box."

Eventually, the cars made their way to the grid, all spotless in presentation. The Bugatti drivers had their names emblazoned on the scuttles of their cars in brilliant silver, whilst the Auto Unions proudly bore swastikas on their tails. The very mixed grid formed up.

"Hans Stuck (Auto Union A-type) and Achille Varzi (Scuderia Ferrari Alfa Romeo) made up the front row; behind

The 1934 Grand Prix, and the twin Mercedes W25s of Rudolf Carraciola (leading) and Luigi Fagioli show the way to Hans Stuck's Auto Union A-type. The corner is Virage de la Ferme.

them were Rudolf Carraciola (Mercedes Benz W25), Momberger (Auto Union), and Chiron (Alfa). Tazio Nuvolari was the first of the Bugattis; behind him sat Benoist and Dreyfus in similar cars. Toward the back of the grid Trossi (Alfa), von Brauchtisch (Mercedes), Zehander (Maserati), and Etancelin (Maserati) were in front of last placed man Luigi Fagioli in the third Mercedes."

Mercedes was the strong favourite, its new W25 Silver Arrows showing "... terrific speed ..." in practice, as did the Auto Unions, although they had been been rather unreliable. Of the rest only the Ferrari-run Alfas seemed capable of even coming close to the Silver dream racers.

"Two minutes to two. As far as the eye could see the grounds, stands, trees, the landscape generally were black with people seething with excitement, concentrated on those thirteen brightly coloured silent cars. The discipline was magnificent. One-and-a-half minutes to go: not a sound, not a movement. One minute. Every mechanic swung his car's starting handle.

"In one glorious growl of sound the racing cars sprang to life.

"A high official of the ACF, prompted by the timekeeper, raised the club's blue flag. The power of many hundred horses welled up in a fierce scream of noise. Four seconds, two, one ... Quite deliberately, it seemed, Chiron's scarlet Alfa moved from

Autodrome de Linas-Montlhéry

GRAND PRIX DE L'AGE D'OR

40ème édition
80 ans du circuit

19 & 20 juin 2004
dernière ...

Venez voir courir l'histoire

2€

the third row, the flag hesitated, dropped. Chiron went straight by as the twelve other cars went off in a wall of sound."

The race was under way and the silver cars began to hunt down Chiron's scarlet car which led. The Auto Union of Hans Stuck was in the lead by the third lap, the Alfa some way behind with a Mercedes in hot pursuit. Perhaps it was the hot weather, perhaps it was the new technology, or something else entirely but, one-by-one, the cars began dropping out. Momberger went first on lap 10 with steering problems on his Auto Union; the following lap claimed Etancelin and von Brauchtisch, then more dropped out between laps 14 and 17. The Bugatti shared by Wimille and Nuvolari was gone as were the rest of the Mercedes team, Caracciola and Fagioli. Hans Stuck lasted longer but dropped out on the 32nd tour as did Zehender on the following lap. Benoist was running at the finish but was not classified.

"The Scuderia Ferrari Alfa Romeo team of Chiron, Varzi and the partnership of Trossi and Moll finished the race in that order. Once the Alfas had seized control the race became rather devoid of entertainment so the crowd made its own, greeting the arrival of ministers of the French government with a stupendous chorus of shrieks, howls and whistling in response to extra taxes they had imposed. The five or so minutes before the cars came around again were enlivened by one gentleman dropping a flaming cigarette lighter down the back of another, the fire brigade rushing to deal with the resultant complication."

The circuit continued in use right up until the war, when, for reasons of occupation, it became inactive, though the last Grand Prix had been run there in 1937. Following the war the circuit returned to action whilst Brooklands was left to rot, leased to the Union Technique de l'Automobile du Motorcycle et du Cycle (UTAC) on a long term basis. The handover took place in December 1946. The track was renovated over the following two years, a control tower was added, plus a 1000 seater stand and fuelling area, and parts of the venue were converted for use as a vehicle proving ground, which has mainly occupied the track to the present day.

There was a lot more racing to be enjoyed, however, and for many years during the Paris Motor Show the Coupes du Salon was run, and another major event was the 1000km de Paris,

which ran on an irregular basis from 1956 to 2004, latterly in abbreviated form.

In more recent years the Grand Prix de l'Age d'Or – an historic festival celebrating the circuit's past and recreating the 1000km de Paris – was added to the calendar. In April 2001 the National Speed Commission renewed the circuit's permit to allow racing until 2004. The permit will not be renewed again.

Over the years modifications have been made to the track: chicanes were added at the base of the banking, and also just after the road course rejoins the Piste de Vitesse; links were built between the two legs of the road course at Deux Ponts, Couard, Côte Lapize (near Gendarme), and a new corner built after Bruyères, Virage Caroline, a fast right-hand sweep that bypasses the Biscornes section, named for a young lady who died there in 1961. These links give numerous circuit layout options.

… and now

A reasonably large crowd turned up for the 2004 Grand Prix de l'Age d'Or and was rewarded with huge grids full of a wide variety of historic racing cars. The access road was jammed back onto the main road out of Paris. On-track action was plentiful, especially along the start/finish straight, which, in its final form, was very wide indeed at one end, and ultra-narrow at the other. The bottleneck grid caused chaos at the start of one 44 car race, with 5 cars involved in a mini pile-up. In a later race a monumental duel took place between two huge Bentleys. No-one cared that these were the two slowest cars on the track and there seemed never much more than an inch between them; sometimes they were line astern, sometimes abreast. Then, halfway through the race the big Bentleys peeled into the pits and pulled up line astern. Both drivers leapt out of their cars, the lead car taken over by its second driver. To ensure a fair fight the driver of the second car ran around it before jumping back in. The two Bentleys pulled out of the pits and resumed their scrap. Throughout the entire race, including the events in the pits, the action didn't abate. It was the last great motor racing battle the circuit would ever see.

Great battles and great cars, there's no doubt this was one of the circuit's greatest days. Stirling Moss drove demonstration runs, and Steve McQueen's Porsche 908 was raced against Lola T70s and a brutal Corvette in the 1000km de Paris. Barbecues and reminiscences rounded off each day.

On the final day of the meeting the last race was run as the sun was setting. This was not simply the end of just another Parisian weekend, nor the end of an era, but the end of a life. This circuit lived.

The Virage Caroline had a strange atmosphere, slightly ominous. Maybe it was the oppressive presence of an Army depot, or simply the deserted nature of the area. It was very, very quiet, a birdless grove. Back up on the autodrome section the final car races ran, and every now and then a burst of rather shocking noise shattered the unnatural silence.

Today, the circuit is mostly intact. Faded adverts adorn the pit and start areas, the pit counter remains unchanged but, again, run down. The two great bankings are there but stained with rust from the barriers at the top; in places repairs give a patchwork quilt effect. Out on the road course part of the Biscornes loop has been obliterated by the construction of a barracks, the other leg blocked off by a large metal gate. The kerbing paint is faded and flaking, the red pigment has bleached to pink. The track surface is scarred by cracks and bumps, and tyre walls have become overgrown with flowering weeds.

Another one; the small stone bearing the name of a dead racer, is tucked down in grass that is slowly overgrowing it. Along the edge of the track, spaced apart almost evenly as if by design, lay monuments to the fallen. The drone in the background is familiar, but very distant, like an intruder, an intruder in a cemetery. We stand back and look and wonder just how this rider lost his life; you want to lay flowers by the stone – somebody should – but few notice these little stones by the side of the track. We move on as, in the distance, another race starts. Something dark lies in the grass at the side of the track on the far side about twenty metres away. Another one …

Linas is a time capsule; a tragic reminder of the past. It would take huge investment for racing to return to the full course as the banking is crumbling, chunks of concrete have fallen and now litter the underside. Linas no longer has a motor racing circuit; does anyone in the town care? They still have a kart track, after all …

JAGUAR RECORD RUN
SEVEN DAYS AND SEVEN NIGHTS AT OVER 100mph

HENRY DE COURCELLES
2 JUILLET 1927

G. MAIRESSE

ROLLAND 1935 196
CHAMPION DE FRANCE

Appendix

Motel Avus,
Halenseestrasse 51,
Berlin,
Germany

Brooklands Museum,
Brooklands Road,
Weybridge,
Surrey,KT13 0QN,
England
http://www.brooklandsmuseum.com/

Crystal Palace Museum,
Anerley Hill,
London SE19 2BA,
England
http://www.crystalpalacefoundation.org.uk/

Monza,
Autodromo Nazionale Monza,
via Vedano 5,
20052 Monza (MI),
Italy
http://www.monzanet.it

Nürburgring
Nürburgring GmbH,
Otto-Flimm-Straße,
D - 53520 Nürburg,
Germany
http://www.nuerburgring.de/

Reims-Gueux
A.C.G.
18 Avenue de la gare,
51390 Gueux,
France
http://acg.site.voila.fr/

Keimola
http://personal.inet.fi/urheilu/keimola/

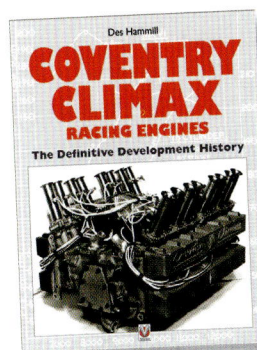

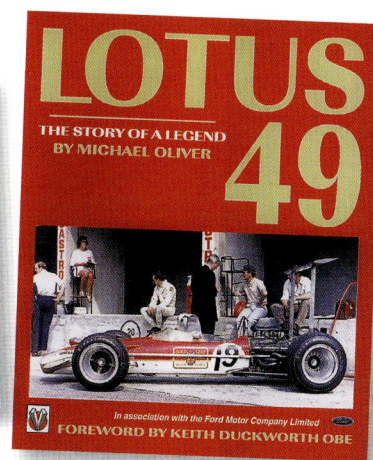

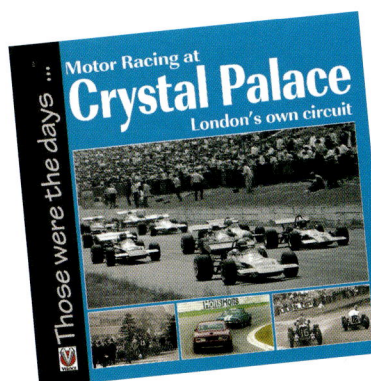

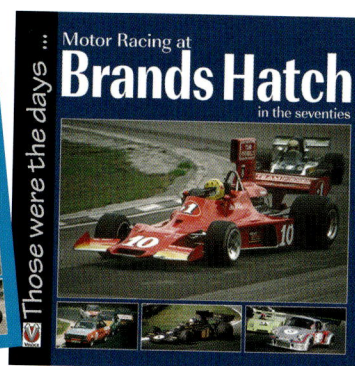

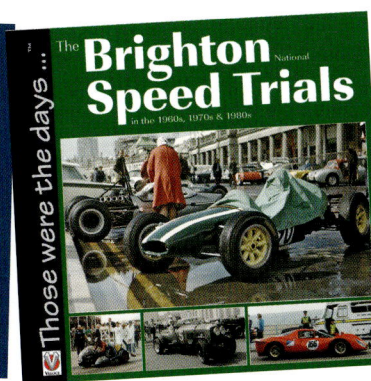

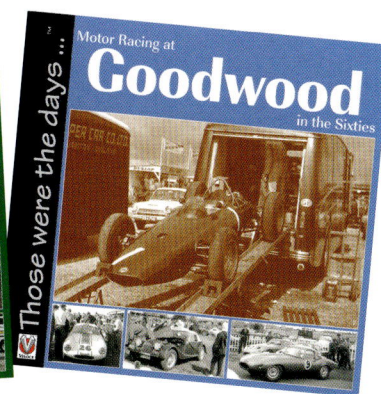

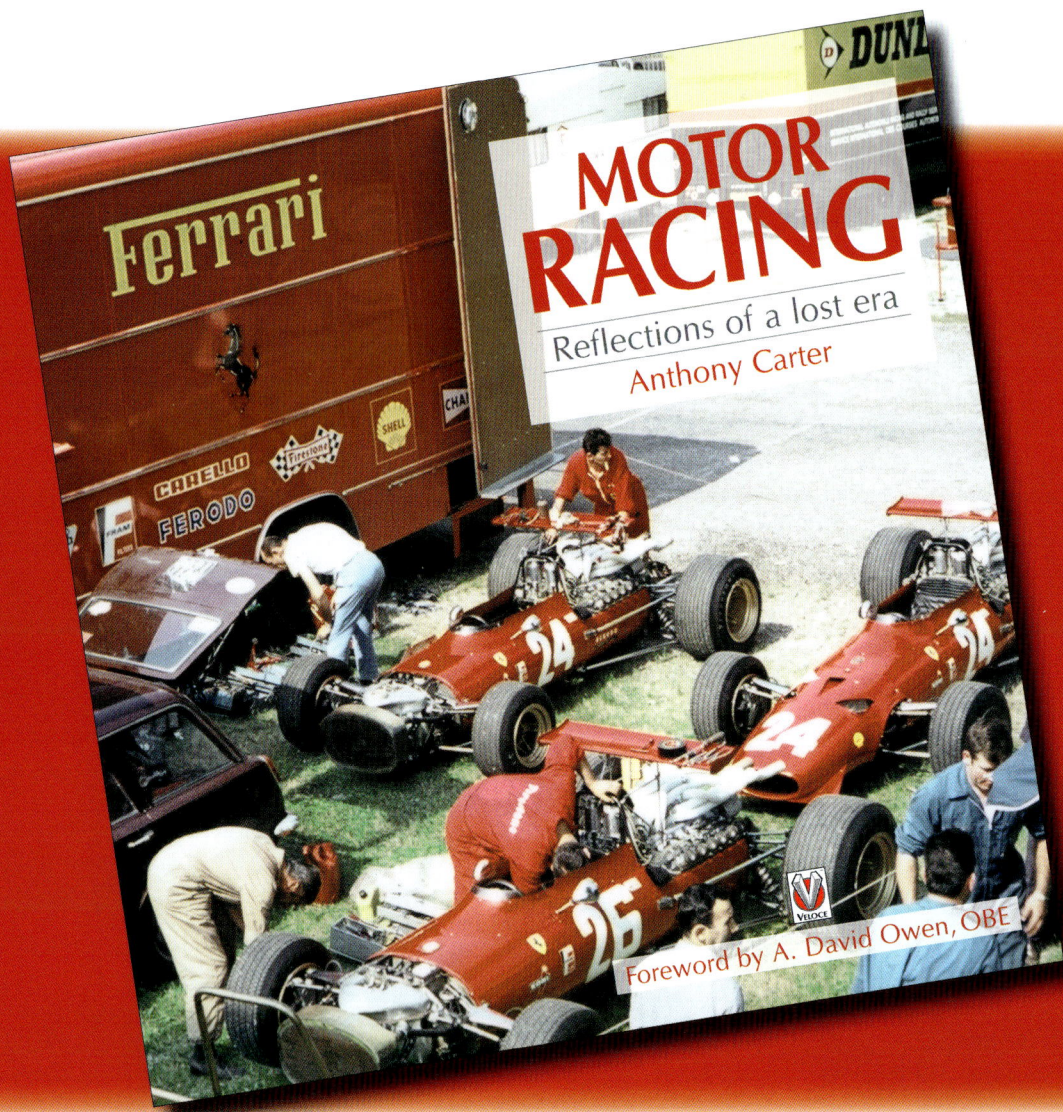

MOTOR RACING

Reflections of a lost era

Anthony Carter

Cloth hardback
192 pages
Over 300 colour/b&w photos
ISBN: 1904788106
£49.99*

*price subject to change
please call for p&p: 01305 260068

A nostalgic trip back to an era of motor racing in Great Britain and Europe when the sport was less commercial, much more accessible, and much more dangerous.

The period covered – 1956 to 1979 – saw the end of the front engined Grand Prix cars spawned by the behemoths of the vintage period, and ushered in a new breed of elegant, lightweight, rear engined cars, whose genes are still very evident in today's F1 racers. This was also the era of the great sports racing cars from a myriad of manufacturers.

This really is an extraordinary book. You will not have seen before the photographs it contains: they were all taken by the author, without the benefit of a press pass or special access, and were never intended to be published. Over 300 delightfully spontaneous and opportunistic pictures in colour and monochrome – rediscovered in the attic during a house move – show just how easy it was for an enthusiastic spectator to get close to the cars, drivers and team crew in this period of motorsport. Unusually for a motor racing book, the images are mainly of paddock scenes and the people – drivers, mechanics, course officials, even the man who painted the racing numbers on the cars – preparing for action behind the scenes.

Accompanying his pictures, Anthony's writing brings the era to life again. Colourful and emotive descriptions, and personal recollections allow you to share the author's motor racing experiences so intimately that you might even hear the roar of exhausts and smell the Castrol R in the air ... Enjoy!

Covers the period 1956 to 1979
Over 300 previously unpublished photographs

Index